High Paying AI Proof Jobs

Secure Your Future with Careers That Artificial Intelligence Cannot Replace and Learn the Skills You Need for an AI Resistant Job Market

Harper Wells

Life Level Up Books

Contents

Understanding AI and Its Implications for Everyday Life

A rtificial Intelligence (AI) has made significant strides in recent years, transforming from a theoretical concept into a practical tool integrated into various aspects of daily life. The capabilities of AI today extend far beyond simple automation; it now encompasses a diverse range of applications that enhance efficiency and productivity across multiple sectors.

Overview of AI's Current Capabilities

AI systems are designed to mimic human intelligence by learning from data and making decisions with minimal human intervention. The core capabilities of AI include:

- **Data Analysis**: AI can process vast amounts of data at unprecedented speeds, identifying patterns and trends that would be impossible for humans to detect in a reasonable timeframe.

- **Predictive Analytics**: By analyzing historical data, AI can forecast future trends and outcomes, enabling proactive decision-making.

- **Natural Language Processing (NLP)**: This allows AI to understand, interpret, and generate human language, facilitating more intuitive interactions between humans and machines.

- **Computer Vision**: AI can interpret visual information from the world, enabling applications like facial recognition and autonomous vehicles.

Examples of Tasks AI Can Automate

The automation capabilities of AI have revolutionized numerous tasks traditionally performed by humans. Some notable examples include:

- **Customer Service**: Chatbots powered by NLP can handle customer inquiries 24/7, providing instant responses and freeing up human agents for more complex issues.

- **Manufacturing**: Robots equipped with machine learning algorithms can perform repetitive tasks with high precision, increasing production efficiency and reducing errors.

- **Healthcare**: AI systems can analyze medical images faster than radiologists, identifying abnormalities that might be missed by the human eye.

- **Finance**: Algorithms can automate trading strategies based on real-time market data, execute transactions at optimal times, and manage risk more effectively.

Impact on Productivity in Various Sectors

The integration of AI into different industries has significantly boosted productivity:

- **Retail**: Personalized recommendations powered by AI increase sales by suggesting products that customers are likely to purchase based on their browsing history and past purchases.

- **Transportation**: Autonomous vehicles reduce the need for human drivers, potentially decreasing accident rates caused by human error and improving traffic flow efficiency.

- **Agriculture**: Drones equipped with computer vision technology monitor crop health and optimize irrigation schedules, leading to higher yields and reduced resource waste.

In healthcare, the impact is profound. AI-driven diagnostic tools enhance the accuracy of disease detection. For instance:

> "IBM's Watson Health employs advanced algorithms to assist doctors in diagnosing conditions with remarkable precision."

Such improvements lead to better patient outcomes and more efficient use of medical resources.

Finance is another sector experiencing a transformation due to AI. Automated trading systems not only increase the speed and accuracy of transactions but also help in managing risks associated with market fluctuations. Fraud detection systems powered by machine learning algorithms identify suspicious activities in real-time, safeguarding financial assets.

In manufacturing, the deployment of robotic systems has streamlined production lines. These robots work tirelessly without fatigue, ensuring consistent quality and reducing downtime.

Real-Life Example

Consider the case of Amazon's warehouses where robots work alongside humans. These robots transport goods across vast areas quickly and efficiently. As a result:

1. Human workers are relieved from physically demanding tasks

2. Inventory management becomes more precise

3. Order fulfillment times are drastically reduced

This synergy between human intellect and machine efficiency epitomizes the transformative power of current AI capabilities.

AI has evolved from being a mere assistant to becoming an indispensable asset across various domains. Its ability to automate tasks enhances productivity while its analytical prowess drives informed decision-making processes.

Machine Learning and Deep Learning: The Core of AI

Definitions and Differences Between Machine Learning and Deep Learning

Machine learning (ML) and deep learning (DL) are often used interchangeably, yet they possess distinct characteristics. **Machine learning** is a subset of AI that enables systems to learn from data patterns without explicit programming. Algorithms in ML can be supervised, where the system is trained on labeled data, or unsupervised, where it identifies hidden patterns in unlabeled data.

Deep learning, a specialized branch of ML, uses artificial neural networks with multiple layers—hence the term "deep." These networks mimic the human brain's structure and function, allowing them to process vast amounts of unstructured data like images, audio, and text. While ML can handle simpler tasks efficiently, DL excels in complex pattern recognition due to its depth and capability for abstraction.

Real-Life Applications of These Technologies

The practical applications of machine learning and deep learning span numerous fields:

- **Healthcare**: ML algorithms analyze patient data to predict disease outbreaks or personalize treatment plans. DL models assist in diagnosing medical conditions through image recognition in radiology.

- **Finance**: Fraud detection systems employ ML to identify unusual transaction patterns. In trading, DL algorithms analyze market data for predictive analytics.

- **Retail**: Personalized recommendations based on user behavior are powered by ML. Inventory management leverages these technologies for demand forecasting.

- **Autonomous Vehicles**: Self-driving cars utilize DL for object detection and decision-making processes, ensuring safer navigation.

- **Entertainment**: Streaming services deploy DL to curate personalized content suggestions by analyzing viewing habits.

Importance in AI Development

The significance of machine learning and deep learning in AI development cannot be overstated:

1. **Data Utilization**: Both technologies enable the efficient use of large datasets. As the volume of data grows exponentially, their ability to discern valuable insights becomes critical.

2. **Automation**: Routine tasks across various sectors can be automated, leading to increased productivity and cost savings.

3. **Innovation Catalyst**: By enabling rapid iteration and experimentation, ML and DL drive innovation in emerging fields such as biotechnology or renewable energy.

4. **Enhanced Decision-Making**: Data-driven insights provided by these technologies enhance decision-making processes across industries.

Utilizing these advanced algorithms transforms how businesses operate and interact with customers. The ability to predict trends, understand user preferences, and automate complex tasks exemplifies the transformative potential of machine learning and deep learning.

> "Deep learning is not just about training a neural network; it's about understanding how we can make computers think more like humans." — Geoffrey Hinton

Machine learning and deep learning form the backbone of modern AI advancements. Their capabilities extend beyond mere automation into realms requiring nuanced understanding and predictive power. As these technologies evolve, they promise to unlock new potentials across various sectors, driving both efficiency and innovation.

Natural Language Processing: AI Understanding Human Language

What is Natural Language Processing (NLP)?

Natural language processing (NLP) is a fascinating blend of linguistics, computer science, and artificial intelligence. It enables machines to understand, interpret, and generate human language in a way that is both meaningful and useful. NLP uses algorithms to analyze the structure and meaning of human speech and text, allowing computers to efficiently process large amounts of language data.

Key Components of NLP

Some key components of NLP include:

- **Tokenization**: Breaking down text into smaller units such as words or phrases.

- **Part-of-Speech Tagging**: Identifying the grammatical category of each word.

- **Named Entity Recognition (NER)**: Detecting proper names, dates, locations, etc.

- **Sentiment Analysis**: Determining the emotional tone behind words.

How is NLP Used in Chatbots and Virtual Assistants?

NLP has transformed how we interact with technology through chatbots and virtual assistants. These systems use natural language understanding (NLU) to analyze user input, drawing on extensive datasets to provide relevant responses.

Chatbots

Chatbots serve various roles across different industries:

1. **Customer Service**: Automating responses to common in-

quiries in e-commerce.

2. **Healthcare**: Providing preliminary medical advice based on symptom descriptions.

3. **Finance**: Assisting with transactions and account information.

Virtual Assistants

Virtual assistants like Apple's Siri, Google Assistant, and Amazon's Alexa have become household staples. These tools perform tasks ranging from setting reminders to controlling smart home devices—all through voice commands.

Challenges in Understanding Human Language Nuances

Despite its impressive capabilities, NLP faces significant challenges in fully grasping the nuances of human language. Understanding context, emotion, sarcasm, and cultural references requires a level of sophistication that current AI models are still striving to achieve.

Ambiguity

Human languages are inherently ambiguous:

- **Polysemy**: Words with multiple meanings can confuse AI. For example, "bank" could mean the financial institution or the side of a river.

- **Homophones**: Words that sound identical but have different meanings (e.g., "their" vs. "there").

Contextual Understanding

AI often struggles with maintaining context over extended conversations or texts:
- A statement like "He is too close" can have different interpretations based on prior sentences or situational context.

Sarcasm and Humor

Detecting sarcasm and humor presents another hurdle:
- Phrases like "Great job!" can be sincere or sarcastic depending on tone and situational cues.

The Future of NLP

Addressing these challenges is crucial for advancing NLP technologies. Innovations such as transformers—used in models like GPT-3—are pushing the boundaries by improving context retention and semantic understanding. Continuous research aims to make AI more adept at mimicking the intricacies of human communication.

Understanding natural language processing not only highlights AI's current capabilities but also underscores the complexities involved in bridging the gap between human thought processes and machine interpretation. The journey towards seamless human-AI interaction continues to evolve with every technological breakthrough.

Computer Vision: How AI Sees the World

Overview of Computer Vision Technology

Computer vision is a major advancement in artificial intelligence that allows machines to understand and interpret visual information from the world. It works similarly to human vision, processing images to make decisions or perform tasks without human involvement. The main aspects of computer vision are image recognition, object detection, and scene understanding.

- **Image Recognition**: Identifies objects, people, places, and actions in images.

- **Object Detection**: Locates the presence of objects within an image.

- **Scene Understanding**: Analyzes an entire scene to comprehend context and relationships between objects.

Computer vision uses complex algorithms and deep learning models to analyze visual data. These models are trained on large datasets containing millions of labeled images, allowing them to recognize patterns and features with impressive accuracy.

Applications in Various Industries

Security

In the field of security, computer vision improves surveillance systems by providing real-time monitoring and analysis. Traditional cameras only record footage passively, but with computer vision, these systems can actively identify suspicious activities and notify authorities instantly.

- **Facial Recognition**: Security agencies use facial recognition technology to identify individuals in public areas.

- **Intrusion Detection**: Advanced algorithms can detect unauthorized access or suspicious behavior in restricted spaces.

- **Automated Monitoring**: AI-powered cameras can continuously scan environments, reducing the need for constant human supervision.

Healthcare

Computer vision has brought about significant changes in healthcare, especially in diagnostics and patient care. AI-driven image analysis assists medical professionals in accurately identifying diseases.

- **Radiology**: Automated analysis of X-rays, CT scans, and MRIs helps radiologists find abnormalities like tumors or fractures.

- **Surgical Assistance**: Computer vision supports surgeons by offering real-time guidance during intricate procedures.

- **Remote Monitoring**: Patients can be monitored remotely through video feeds analyzed by AI for signs of distress or unusual behavior.

Retail

Retailers use computer vision to improve customer experience and streamline operations. Visual data collected from stores is analyzed to optimize product placement and enhance inventory management.

- **Customer Insights**: Heatmaps generated from video feeds show customer movement patterns, helping retailers arrange products more effectively.

- **Inventory Management**: Automated systems track stock levels in real-time, reducing instances of overstocking or shortages.

- **Loss Prevention**: AI monitors store activity to detect theft or fraud attempts.

Challenges in Computer Vision

Despite its impressive capabilities, computer vision faces several challenges:

1. **Data Quality**: High-quality annotated data is crucial for training accurate models. Poorly labeled or biased data can lead to erroneous outcomes.

2. **Complexity of Visual Data**: Variations in lighting, angles, occlusions, and background clutter pose significant hurdles.

3. **Ethical Considerations**: Privacy concerns arise when deploying facial recognition technologies in public spaces without consent.

Looking Ahead

Advancements in computer vision continue at a rapid pace. Innovations such as 3D visualization and augmented reality promise to further expand the horizons of this technology. As AI systems become more skilled at interpreting visual data, their applications will undoubtedly spread into even more areas of daily life and industry practices.

Understanding how machines see the world through computer vision offers a glimpse into the future where AI not only enhances human abilities but also operates independently across various sectors. This technology showcases the profound impact AI has on modern society while emphasizing the ongoing need for ethical considerations and robust data practices to ensure its responsible implementation.

AI in Healthcare: Diagnostics, Treatment, and Beyond

Artificial Intelligence (AI) is changing the healthcare industry by improving the accuracy of diagnoses and optimizing treatment plans. **AI healthcare applications** are no longer a futuristic concept but a present reality, transforming how we approach medical challenges.

How AI Improves Diagnostics and Treatment

AI's ability to process large amounts of data leads to significant advancements in diagnostics. Machine learning algorithms can analyze medical images with remarkable precision, identifying patterns that may elude even the most experienced radiologists. Here are some areas where AI is making a difference:

1. Radiology

AI systems have shown the capability to detect abnormalities in X-rays, MRIs, and CT scans more quickly and accurately than traditional methods.

2. Pathology

Deep learning models can examine tissue samples to identify cancerous cells, providing faster results and reducing human error.

3. Genomics

AI helps in interpreting complex genetic data, enabling personalized treatment strategies based on an individual's unique genetic makeup.

By using these capabilities, healthcare providers can make informed decisions, leading to better patient outcomes. As Dr. Eric Topol puts it:

> "AI won't replace doctors, but doctors who use AI will replace those who don't."

How AI Benefits Personalized Medicine

Personalized medicine—tailoring medical treatment to individual characteristics—benefits immensely from AI integration. Here's how:

1. Predictive Analytics

Algorithms analyze patient history and lifestyle factors to predict potential health issues before they manifest.

2. Drug Development

AI speeds up drug discovery by predicting which compounds will be effective against specific diseases, significantly shortening development timelines.

3. Treatment Optimization

Machine learning models recommend treatments based on the patient's unique profile, increasing effectiveness and minimizing side effects.

One compelling example is IBM Watson Health's collaboration with leading oncologists. By processing vast datasets of medical literature and patient records, Watson provides evidence-based treatment recommendations for cancer patients.

Real-World Examples of AI in Healthcare

Several real-world applications illustrate the transformative potential of AI in healthcare:

- **Google's DeepMind Health**: Utilizes deep learning to analyze eye scans accurately, diagnosing conditions like diabetic retinopathy and age-related macular degeneration.

- **PathAI**: Offers advanced pathology solutions that assist pathologists in diagnosing disease with greater accuracy.

- **Tempus**: Combines clinical data with molecular analysis to provide personalized cancer care recommendations.

Challenges of Integrating AI into Healthcare

While the benefits are substantial, integrating AI into healthcare comes with challenges:

- **Data Privacy**: Ensuring patient data confidentiality remains paramount.

- **Bias in Algorithms**: Addressing biases that may arise from training data that does not adequately represent diverse populations.

- **Regulatory Hurdles**: Navigating complex regulatory environments to ensure compliance with healthcare standards.

The ongoing evolution of AI technologies promises to further enhance its contributions to healthcare. As these systems become more sophisticated, their impact on diagnostics and treatment plans will likely grow exponentially.

By understanding these applications and challenges, stakeholders can better navigate this rapidly changing landscape. The journey towards fully integrating AI into healthcare is just beginning, with countless innovations yet to be realized.

AI in Finance: Trading, Risk Management, and Fraud Detection

Artificial intelligence (AI) is transforming the finance industry by changing how trading strategies are created and how risks are managed. With the help of complex algorithms and machine learning techniques, AI applications in finance are making traditional financial processes faster and more precise.

Improving Trading Strategies with AI

AI-driven trading algorithms have become essential in today's finance world. They quickly analyze large amounts of data, finding patterns and trends that human traders might overlook. These algorithms can:

- Execute trades within milliseconds based on market conditions.

- Predict future price movements using historical data.

- Adjust strategies in real-time to optimize profits.

For example, *high-frequency trading (HFT)* firms use AI to make trades at incredibly fast speeds. Being able to process and respond to information quicker than competitors gives them a significant advantage in the fast-moving stock market. Goldman Sachs, a leading investment bank, has incorporated AI into its trading operations, reducing the number of human traders while improving overall efficiency through automated systems.

Reinventing Risk Management Practices

Risk management is another important area where AI shows its worth. Traditional methods of assessing risk often depend on past data and statistical models that may not accurately reflect current market conditions. On the other hand, AI-powered risk management systems continuously learn from new data inputs, adapting to emerging risks more effectively.

Key benefits include:

- **Real-time risk assessment:** Continuous monitoring of market conditions allows for instant adjustments to portfolios.

- **Predictive analytics:** Identifies potential risks before they materialize.

- **Stress testing:** Simulates various scenarios to understand potential impacts on assets and investments.

JPMorgan Chase uses AI to improve its risk management framework. Their system employs machine learning models to analyze transactions and identify anomalies that could indicate potential risks. This proactive approach enables the bank to address threats before they escalate into major problems.

Using AI for Fraud Detection Systems

Fraud detection is an ongoing challenge in the finance industry. As fraudulent activities become more sophisticated, traditional methods of detection often fall short. This is where AI comes into play with its ability to sift through massive amounts of data to identify unusual patterns indicative of fraud.

AI-based fraud detection systems offer several advantages:

- **Anomaly detection:** Machine learning models can spot deviations from normal behavior that may indicate fraudulent activity.

- **Behavioral analysis:** Understanding typical user behavior helps in distinguishing between legitimate transactions and potential fraud.

- **Adaptive learning:** Systems evolve as new fraud techniques emerge, maintaining their effectiveness over time.

A notable example is PayPal's use of AI for fraud detection. Their system analyzes millions of transactions daily, using deep learning techniques to identify suspicious activities with high accuracy. This proactive stance not only protects consumers but also enhances trust in digital payment platforms.

Wider Implications for Financial Institutions

The integration of AI into finance goes beyond just trading, risk management, and fraud detection. It creates a stronger financial ecosystem that can quickly respond to changes in the market and new threats. Financial institutions that embrace these technologies gain a competitive edge through improved operational efficiency and better decision-making abilities.

As technology continues to advance, the relationship between finance and AI will grow stronger, leading to innovations that reshape financial services in a dynamic and sustainable way.

AI in Retail: Personalization, Inventory Management, and Sales

The retail sector is undergoing a transformative revolution, driven by the potent capabilities of artificial intelligence (AI). This change is not just about enhancing operations but reshaping the entire consumer experience. Let's delve into how AI is making waves in personalization, inventory management, and sales.

Personalization: Crafting Unique Customer Experiences

AI's role in personalization has become indispensable. By leveraging vast amounts of customer data, AI algorithms can:

- **Analyze purchase history and browsing behavior:** Retailers can predict what products a customer might be interested in next.

- **Recommend products tailored to individual preferences:** This increases the likelihood of conversions and enhances customer satisfaction.

- **Personalize marketing campaigns:** Targeted advertisements based on AI analytics ensure that customers receive relevant promotions.

For instance, Amazon's recommendation engine is a classic example of AI-driven personalization. It uses collaborative filtering and deep learning techniques to suggest items that align with a user's past interactions.

Inventory Management: Enhancing Efficiency and Reducing Costs

Efficient inventory management is crucial for any retailer. AI offers remarkable tools to optimize this aspect:

- **Predictive analytics:** AI can forecast demand for products based on historical data and current market trends.

- **Automated restocking:** By predicting when stock levels are low, AI systems can automate orders from suppliers.

- **Reducing waste:** Predictive models help minimize overstocking or understocking, leading to cost savings and reduced waste.

Zara employs an advanced AI system that analyzes sales data and fashion trends to make real-time adjustments to its inventory. This agility allows Zara to respond swiftly to changing consumer demands.

Sales Optimization: Maximizing Revenue Opportunities

AI is not just about managing backend operations; it significantly impacts front-end sales strategies too:

- **Dynamic pricing models:** AI algorithms adjust prices based on demand fluctuations, competitor pricing, and other external factors.

- **Customer sentiment analysis:** By analyzing reviews and social media mentions, AI helps retailers understand customer sentiment towards their products.

- **Sales forecasting:** Accurate predictions of future sales enable better planning and strategy formulation.

A notable example is Walmart's utilization of machine learning models to set competitive prices dynamically. These models consider various factors such as time of day, product demand, and competitor pricing, ensuring optimal sales performance.

Real-Life Applications: Bridging Theory and Practice

Several real-life applications underscore the profound impact of AI in retail:

- **Sephora's Virtual Artist**Utilizes computer vision technology to allow customers to try on makeup virtually.

- Provides personalized product recommendations based on facial features.

- **H&M's Data-Driven Design**Analyzes social media trends and customer feedback to design clothing lines that resonate with current fashion preferences.

- Utilizes AI to predict which styles will be popular in upcoming seasons.

- **Macy's On Call**An AI-powered mobile tool that assists customers with store navigation.

- Provides instant answers about product availability and store policies through natural language processing (NLP).

The Road Ahead: Growing Integration and Innovation

As the retail landscape continues to evolve, the integration of AI will only deepen. Future innovations may include:

- Enhanced virtual reality (VR) shopping experiences powered by AI.

- More sophisticated chatbots capable of handling complex customer queries seamlessly.

- Advanced fraud detection mechanisms protecting both retailers and consumers.

In essence, the synergy between artificial intelligence and retail holds immense potential—transforming traditional methods into cutting-edge strategies that drive growth, efficiency, and unparalleled customer satisfaction.

Autonomous Vehicles: The Future of Transportation

Autonomous vehicles, often referred to as self-driving cars, represent a groundbreaking shift in how we perceive and utilize transportation. This technological marvel promises to revolutionize daily commutes, logistics, and even urban planning.

Understanding Autonomous Vehicles

At the core of autonomous vehicles is a complex interplay of *sensors, algorithms,* and *machine learning.* These vehicles are equipped with:

- **Lidar**: Measures distances using laser light to create precise

3D maps of the environment.

- **Radar**: Utilizes radio waves to detect objects' speed and movement.

- **Cameras**: Capture real-time images to identify road signs, traffic lights, and obstacles.

- **Ultrasonic Sensors**: Detect close-range obstacles for functions like parking assistance.

These sensors feed data into sophisticated algorithms that interpret the vehicle's surroundings, allowing it to navigate safely without human intervention.

Real-World Applications and Benefits

Autonomous vehicles have already made significant strides in various sectors:

Ride-Hailing Services

Companies like Waymo and Uber are testing self-driving taxis in select cities. These services aim to reduce wait times and provide an efficient mode of transport.

> "The future belongs to those who believe in the beauty of their dreams." - Eleanor Roosevelt

Freight and Logistics

Self-driving trucks are being tested for long-haul routes. This innovation could lead to more reliable deliveries and reduced operational costs. Imagine a fleet of trucks that can operate 24/7 without fatigue.

Public Transportation

Autonomous buses are being piloted in urban areas. These buses promise smoother rides with optimized routes based on real-time traffic data.

Safety and Efficiency

One of the most compelling arguments for autonomous vehicles is enhanced safety. Human errors cause over 90% of road accidents. Autonomous vehicles, with their ability to process vast amounts of data instantaneously, can react faster than any human driver. For instance:

- **Collision Avoidance**: Advanced algorithms can predict potential collisions and take preemptive actions.

- **Adaptive Cruise Control**: Maintains a safe distance from other vehicles by adjusting speed automatically.

The efficiency aspect cannot be overlooked either. Autonomous vehicles can communicate with each other through Vehicle-to-Vehicle (V2V) communication, leading to synchronized driving patterns that reduce traffic congestion.

Challenges Ahead

Despite the promising outlook, several challenges need addressing:

1. **Legal and Regulatory Hurdles**: Establishing uniform laws across different regions is crucial for widespread adoption.

2. **Ethical Dilemmas**: Deciding how a vehicle should act in unavoidable accident scenarios raises ethical questions about programming moral decisions.

3. **Technical Limitations**: Adverse weather conditions can impair sensor functionality. Continuous improvements in AI will be necessary to address these limitations.

A Glimpse into the Future

As technology progresses, autonomous vehicles may integrate with smart city infrastructure. Traffic lights could adapt dynamically based on real-time traffic flow, reducing idle time at intersections.

Imagine a future where:

- Parking becomes obsolete as self-driving cars drop passengers off and find remote parking spots autonomously.

- Emissions decrease significantly due to optimized driving patterns.

This vision isn't far-fetched but rather an impending reality shaping our approach to transportation.

The implications for everyday life extend beyond convenience; they touch on safety, efficiency, and environmental impact—ushering us into an era where transportation is not just about getting from point A to point B but doing so intelligently and sustainably.

AI in Entertainment: Content Creation and Personalization

Artificial Intelligence has transformed the entertainment industry, changing how content is created and consumed. With the use of AI technologies, we now have unprecedented levels of personalization and efficiency, greatly impacting our experience with media.

Content Creation

AI algorithms can now create content that was previously only possible through human creativity. From composing music to writing scripts and even creating visual art, AI is expanding the limits of what can be done.

1. Music Composition

Platforms like Amper Music and Jukedeck use AI to compose original music tracks. These tools allow users to specify parameters such as mood, tempo, and genre, resulting in tailor-made compositions. A notable example is the album "I AM AI" by Taryn Southern, entirely composed with the help of an AI.

2. Scriptwriting

ScriptBook offers AI-driven analysis for screenplay writing, providing insights into plot structure, character development, and marketability. This technology can predict box office success and audience reception, giving writers valuable feedback before production begins.

3. Visual Arts

Artbreeder uses machine learning to blend different art styles and create unique images. The technology behind Artbreeder allows artists to explore new creative realms by merging their own work with AI-generated suggestions.

Personalization

The idea of a "one-size-fits-all" approach in entertainment is quickly becoming outdated. Thanks to AI's ability to analyze large amounts of data, we now have highly personalized content recommendations.

1. Streaming Services

Netflix employs sophisticated recommendation algorithms that analyze viewing history, preferences, and even time spent on particular genres to suggest tailored content. This creates a deeply engaging user experience where viewers are continuously introduced to new shows and movies that align with their tastes.

2. Social Media

Platforms like TikTok use machine learning to curate personalized video feeds. By analyzing user interactions—likes, shares, comments—the algorithm fine-tunes content delivery, ensuring each user's feed becomes increasingly relevant over time.

3. Gaming

In video games, AI personalizes experiences by adapting difficulty levels based on player performance. Games like Middle-Earth: Shadow of War use AI-driven systems such as the Nemesis System to create unique interactions with non-playable characters (NPCs), making each player's journey distinct.

Real-Life Applications

AI's presence in entertainment isn't just theoretical; there are real-world examples:

1. **Deepfake Technology**: While often controversial due to ethical implications, deepfake technology demonstrates AI's capability in visual media manipulation. It allows for realistic alterations of video content, raising both creative possibilities and ethical questions within the industry.

2. **Virtual Influencers**: Lil Miquela is a virtual influencer created using AI technologies. With millions of followers on Instagram, she engages in brand endorsements and social causes much like her human counterparts, blurring the lines between reality and virtuality.

3. **Interactive Storytelling**: Netflix's "Bandersnatch," an interactive film from the Black Mirror series, leverages AI to offer multiple narrative paths based on viewer choices. This creates a dynamic storytelling experience where each decision shapes the storyline's outcome.

Challenges

AI's role in entertainment brings up several challenges:

- **Intellectual Property**: Who owns the rights to content created by AI? This question remains largely unresolved within legal frameworks.

- **Authenticity**: Audiences value genuine human creativity; excessive reliance on AI may dilute this authenticity.

- **Bias and Representation**: Algorithms trained on biased datasets can reinforce stereotypes or exclude minority voices from mainstream media.

Looking Ahead

The integration of AI into entertainment marks a new era filled with opportunities and dilemmas alike. As these technologies continue to develop, they promise not only richer but also more complex interactions between creators and audiences. Finding a balance between using AI capabilities while preserving human creativity will be crucial in shaping the future landscape of entertainment.

Smart Home Technology: AI in Daily Life

Smart home technology represents the convergence of artificial intelligence and everyday living. By integrating AI into household devices, our homes have evolved from simple shelters into smart ecosystems that anticipate and cater to our needs.

Voice-Activated Assistants

Voice-activated assistants such as Amazon's Alexa, Google Assistant, and Apple's Siri have become common in many households. These AI-driven entities perform tasks ranging from setting reminders to controlling smart home devices. The convenience they offer cannot be overstated:

- **Hands-free operation:** Users can issue voice commands without interrupting their activities.

- **Integration with other devices:** These assistants sync with smart bulbs, thermostats, and even coffee makers, creating a seamless living experience.

- **Continuous learning:** Over time, these systems learn user preferences, offering tailored suggestions and improving functionality.

Smart Security Systems

Home security has moved beyond traditional alarm systems. Modern smart security solutions use AI for better protection:

- **Facial recognition:** Advanced cameras detect familiar faces and alert homeowners to unknown individuals.

- **Behavioral analysis:** AI algorithms analyze patterns such as usual entry times or frequent visitors, raising alarms for unusual activities.

- **Real-time alerts:** Instant notifications on mobile devices keep users informed of any potential security breaches.

Energy Management

AI-driven smart thermostats like Nest and Ecobee optimize energy consumption by learning user routines and adjusting settings accordingly. This not only reduces utility bills but also promotes environmental sustainability.

- **Adaptive learning:** These systems track heating/cooling preferences and make adjustments to maximize comfort while minimizing energy use.

- **Remote access:** Users can control their energy settings via smartphone apps, ensuring efficiency even when away from home.

- **Predictive maintenance:** Some systems can alert users to potential HVAC issues before they become costly repairs.

Smart Appliances

The kitchen has also embraced the smart home trend:

- **Connected refrigerators:** These appliances monitor food inventory, suggest recipes based on available ingredients, and notify users when items are running low.

- **AI ovens:** Intelligent ovens recognize different foods and automatically set optimal cooking temperatures and times.

- **Robot vacuums:** Devices such as Roomba use AI to navigate rooms efficiently, avoid obstacles, and even return to their charging stations autonomously.

Personalized Entertainment

AI personalizes home entertainment by making recommendations based on individual preferences:

- **Streaming services:** Platforms like Netflix and Spotify utilize algorithms to suggest content tailored to user tastes, enhancing the viewing or listening experience.

- **Smart TVs:** These devices integrate with voice assistants, allowing users to search for shows, adjust volume, or switch channels using voice commands.

Health Monitoring

AI-powered health monitoring systems offer several benefits within the home environment:

- **Wearable tech integration:** Devices like Fitbit or Apple Watch can sync with home systems to provide comprehensive health data tracking.

- **Telemedicine capabilities:** Smart mirrors equipped with diagnostic tools allow users to conduct basic health assessments at home.

- **Medication reminders:** AI systems can issue alerts for medication schedules, ensuring adherence to treatment plans.

Challenges in Smart Home Technology

While the benefits are substantial, challenges remain:

Privacy concerns arise due to the extensive data collection inherent in smart home ecosystems. Ensuring robust encryption and secure data handling practices is critical.

Interoperability issues present another hurdle. With countless manufacturers producing various smart devices, achieving seamless integration remains a challenge requiring standardized protocols.

The Future of AI in Smart Homes

The trajectory of smart home technology points toward even greater integration and functionality. Envision homes that not only respond but also predict needs with uncanny accuracy—homes where AI orchestrates every aspect of daily life seamlessly.

Such advancements will undoubtedly redefine convenience while posing new questions about privacy and dependency on technology. As we embrace these innovations, striking a balance between utility and ethical considerations will be paramount.

AI in Education: Personalized Learning and Administration

Artificial Intelligence has brought transformative changes to the education sector. By leveraging AI, educators can cater to individual learning needs, streamline administrative tasks, and enhance the overall educational experience.

Personalized Learning

AI-powered personalized learning systems adapt to each student's unique pace and style of learning. These systems analyze a vast array of data points—from quiz scores to interaction patterns—to create customized educational experiences.

1. Adaptive Learning Platforms

Tools such as DreamBox and Knewton adjust the difficulty of tasks based on real-time analysis of student performance. If a student struggles with a particular concept, the system provides additional resources and exercises targeted at that specific area.

2. Intelligent Tutoring Systems

AI tutors like Carnegie Learning can provide one-on-one support, offering explanations, answering questions, and even predicting where students might struggle next.

3. Feedback Mechanisms

Immediate feedback is crucial for effective learning. Automated grading systems enable teachers to provide rapid feedback on assignments, helping students understand their mistakes and learn from them quickly.

Enhanced Administrative Efficiency

Administrative tasks often consume a significant portion of educators' time. AI solutions can automate many of these tasks, allowing educators to focus more on teaching and student interaction.

1. Automated Scheduling

Systems like SchoolMint use AI to optimize class schedules based on teacher availability, classroom resources, and individual student needs.

2. Enrollment Management

AI-driven platforms streamline the enrollment process by automating application reviews, reducing paperwork, and ensuring compliance with regulations.

3. Resource Allocation

Predictive analytics help schools allocate resources more effectively. For instance, identifying which subjects or activities need more funding or staff based on historical data trends.

Real-Life Applications

Consider the example of Georgia State University. The institution implemented an AI chatbot named "Pounce" to assist with administrative queries. Pounce successfully handled thousands of inquiries about enrollment procedures, financial aid, and more—significantly reducing the workload for human staff.

Another notable example is the use of AI in New York City's public schools. The schools employ machine learning algorithms to predict which students are at risk of dropping out. This early warning system allows administrators to intervene proactively, providing necessary support to keep students engaged.

Challenges in Implementation

Despite its benefits, integrating AI into education comes with challenges:

1. **Data Privacy Concerns**: Collecting and analyzing student data raises significant privacy issues. Schools must ensure robust data protection measures are in place.

2. **Bias in Algorithms**: There is a risk that AI systems could perpetuate existing biases in education if not carefully monitored and adjusted.

3. **Cost Barriers**: Implementing advanced AI solutions can be expensive, posing a challenge for underfunded schools.

Future Prospects

The potential of AI in education appears boundless. Innovations such as virtual reality classrooms powered by AI could offer immersive learning experiences that transcend traditional boundaries. Additionally, advances in natural language processing could lead to more nuanced interactions between students and AI systems.

AI's role in education continues to evolve rapidly, promising a future where tailored learning pathways become the norm rather than the exception.

With these multifaceted applications and considerations, it's clear that AI holds significant promise for revolutionizing educational practices while also presenting new challenges that must be addressed thoughtfully.

Future Capabilities of AI: What's on the Horizon

The rapid evolution of artificial intelligence suggests a future where its capabilities go far beyond today's applications. Looking ahead at these advancements gives us an idea of how AI will soon be present in every part of our lives, changing industries, societies, and personal experiences.

Enhanced Autonomy and Decision-Making

AI's ability to make autonomous decisions is expected to reach unprecedented levels. Imagine systems that not only recommend actions but also execute them with minimal human intervention:

- **Fully autonomous vehicles** navigating complex urban environments without a driver

- **Automated financial advisors** managing investment portfolios with real-time adjustments

- **Smart logistics networks** optimizing routes dynamically

Advanced Human-AI Collaboration

Collaboration between humans and AI will become more seamless and intuitive. Here are some examples:

- **AI-powered exoskeletons** could enhance physical capabilities in industrial settings

- **Intelligent virtual assistants** might predict needs before they arise, offering solutions proactively

The integration of AI into everyday tools will amplify human potential, transforming how we work and interact with technology.

Ubiquitous Personalization

The idea of personalization will take on new dimensions as AI becomes more skilled at understanding individual preferences and behaviors. Consider these scenarios:

- An **education system** where lesson plans are uniquely tailored to each student's learning style

- **Healthcare regimes** that adapt based on continuous monitoring of a patient's condition

This level of personalization could lead to unparalleled efficiency and satisfaction across various domains.

Emotional Intelligence and Empathy

Current AI systems often lack the ability to truly understand human emotions. However, future iterations could incorporate **emotional intelligence**, enabling machines to detect and respond to emotional cues accurately. This development could revolutionize customer service, mental health support, and even personal relationships by providing empathetic interactions that were previously unattainable.

Quantum Computing Synergy

Quantum computing holds the promise of exponentially increasing computational power, which could break through many limitations faced by classical AI algorithms. This synergy might enable breakthroughs in areas such as:

- **Drug discovery:** where simulations of molecular interactions could lead to faster development of new treatments

- **Climate modeling:** providing deeper insights into environmental changes

Ethical AI Development

As AI's capabilities grow, so does the importance of addressing ethical considerations. Future efforts will likely focus on creating transparent algorithms that are free from bias and ensuring privacy protections are robust. The goal is to develop AI that is not only powerful but also aligned with societal values and norms.

Hypothetical Scenarios: A Glimpse into the Future

Here are some hypothetical scenarios showcasing potential future applications of AI:

1. *Healthcare:* Imagine walking into a doctor's office where an AI system analyzes your medical history, current symptoms, and genetic information within seconds to provide a highly accurate diagnosis and treatment plan.

2. *Entertainment:* Envision a world where your favorite TV shows are co-created by AI systems that adapt storylines based on viewer feedback in real-time.

3. *Urban Planning:* Think about cities designed with the help of AI that predicts population growth patterns, traffic flow, and resource needs decades in advance.

Real-World Examples Paving the Way

Innovations today hint at what's possible tomorrow:

- The development of **GPT-3**, an advanced language model by OpenAI, showcases how natural language processing can approach human-like text generation.

- Google's DeepMind has made strides in protein folding prediction with **AlphaFold**, hinting at transformative impacts on biology and medicine.

Looking ahead at these future capabilities invites us to think about not just what technology can achieve but also how it will shape our world. Understanding these possibilities prepares us for a landscape where AI's role is intricately woven into the fabric of everyday life.

Quantum Computing: An Introduction and Its Potential

Quantum computing is a significant change in computer technology, offering the ability to solve problems that classical computers cannot. Unlike traditional bits, which are either 0 or 1, quantum bits or *qubits* can be both at the same time due to a property called superposition. This unique feature greatly increases the potential processing power of quantum computers.

The Fundamentals of Quantum Computing

To fully appreciate the potential of quantum computing, it's important to understand its key principles:

1. **Superposition**: Qubits can exist in multiple states simultaneously, enabling quantum computers to process large amounts of data at once.

2. **Entanglement**: This is when qubits become linked together; the state of one qubit instantly influences the state of another, regardless of how far apart they are.

3. **Quantum Gates**: These are operations performed on qubits that change their state according to the rules of quantum mechanics.

These principles allow quantum computers to solve complex problems more efficiently than classical computers.

Real-World Applications

The real-world possibilities of quantum computing are vast and transformative. Here are some examples:

1. **Cryptography**: Current encryption methods depend on the difficulty of factoring large numbers—a task that could become easy for a quantum computer.

2. **Drug Discovery**: Simulating molecular structures requires a lot of computational power; quantum computers could speed up this process, resulting in quicker drug development.

3. **Optimization Problems**: Industries like logistics and finance deal with complicated optimization challenges that

could be solved more effectively using quantum algorithms.

Hypothetical Scenario: Weather Prediction

Imagine a world where weather patterns can be predicted accurately weeks in advance. Quantum computing could analyze the enormous datasets needed for precise weather modeling much faster than today's supercomputers. This ability would greatly improve agriculture, disaster preparedness, and many other sectors that rely on weather forecasts.

Industry Giants and Quantum Research

Leading companies are driving research and development in quantum computing:

- **IBM**: Created the IBM Q System One, a universal quantum computer available for commercial use.

- **Google**: Announced "quantum supremacy" with its Sycamore processor, solving a problem in 200 seconds that would take classical supercomputers 10,000 years.

- **Microsoft**: Is focusing on topological qubits with the goal of creating more stable and scalable quantum systems.

The Potential Impact on AI

Quantum computing has the potential to significantly impact AI development by processing large datasets more efficiently:

1. **Training Models Faster**: Quantum algorithms could greatly reduce the time it takes to train machine learning models.

2. **Improving Accuracy**: The increased computational power enables the use of more complex models with higher accuracy rates.

3. **Real-Time Data Processing**: This technology could allow for immediate decision-making in areas such as self-driving cars and financial trading.

Challenges Ahead

Despite its potential, there are several obstacles that need to be overcome before quantum computing becomes widely used:

- **Error Rates**: Quantum systems are highly vulnerable to errors caused by decoherence and noise.

- **Scalability**: Creating scalable quantum systems is still a major challenge.

- **Resource Requirements**: Keeping qubits at extremely low temperatures requires advanced cryogenic systems.

Reflecting on the Future

Quantum computing has the potential to transform various industries by providing computational abilities that were previously thought impossible. Its combination with AI holds particular promise for rapid advancements across fields like healthcare and finance.

> "The greatest risk we face is not that our aim is too high and we miss it, but that it is too low and we achieve it." — Michelangelo

By understanding these potentials and challenges, we open up opportunities for a future where technology surpasses current limitations.

Current State of Quantum Computing: Progress and Challenges

Quantum computing is a major advancement over classical computing, using the principles of quantum mechanics to perform complex calculations much faster. However, this significant change comes with its own set of challenges and achievements.

Progress in Quantum Computing

One of the most significant breakthroughs in quantum computing is the achievement of *quantum supremacy*. This milestone was reached when Google's quantum processor, Sycamore, successfully completed a specific task faster than any known classical computer.

Other important advancements include:

- **Quantum Hardware**: Companies like IBM and Intel have developed more advanced quantum processors. For example, IBM's Q System One is a 20-qubit system that is commercially available.

- **Error Correction**: Quantum bits (qubits) are very sensitive to interference from their surroundings. Research into quantum error correction codes is crucial for creating reliable systems. One promising approach is called the Surface Code method.

- **Algorithm Development**: Quantum algorithms such as Shor's algorithm for factoring large numbers and Grover's algorithm for searching databases show potential for practical uses.

Challenges in Quantum Computing

Despite these advancements, there are still several challenges facing the field:

1. **Decoherence and Noise**: Qubits are susceptible to decoherence, which means they can lose their quantum state due to external noise. It remains a significant challenge to keep qubits coherent for longer periods of time.

2. **Scalability**: Building a scalable quantum computer with thousands or millions of qubits requires overcoming major technical obstacles related to qubit connectivity and error rates.

3. **Material Science**: Ongoing research is focused on developing materials that can support stable qubits at higher temperatures (most current systems operate near absolute zero).

4. **Complexity in Algorithms**: While some algorithms show promise, many problems still do not have efficient solutions using quantum methods. Finding innovative approaches and gaining a deeper understanding will be necessary to bridge this gap.

Case Study: IBM Q Network

The IBM Q Network serves as an example of both progress and challenges within the field:

Progress

- Provides cloud-based access to quantum computing resources.

- Collaborates with universities, government agencies, and businesses to explore practical applications.

Challenges

- Ensuring consistent performance across different environments.

- Addressing user demand while maintaining system stability.

"Quantum computers could one day solve problems that are currently unsolvable," says Dario Gil, Director of IBM Research. This optimism highlights both the potential and current limitations faced by researchers.

Real-World Applications Under Exploration

Despite existing challenges, several exciting applications are being explored:

- **Cryptography**: Quantum computers have the potential to break current cryptographic codes but also create new secure encryption methods like Quantum Key Distribution (QKD).

- **Drug Discovery**: More accurate simulations of molecular structures can speed up drug development processes.

- **Optimization Problems**: Logistics companies could transform route optimization using quantum algorithms.

Collaborative Efforts and Future Directions

Global collaboration is crucial for overcoming challenges in quantum computing. Initiatives like the European Union's Quantum Flagship aim to bring together resources from academia, industry, and government.

The way forward includes:

- Investment in *quantum hardware* development.

- Increased focus on *quantum software* engineering.

- Strengthening international *collaborative frameworks*.

These collaborative efforts will be essential as we navigate through the complexities posed by this emerging technology.

Impact of Quantum Computing on AI: Exponential Growth

Quantum computing represents a significant change in computational power, potentially transforming the landscape of artificial intelligence. This technology uses the principles of quantum mechanics to process information in ways that classical computers cannot, promising exponential improvements in AI capabilities.

Unprecedented Speed and Efficiency

Quantum computers operate using **qubits**, which can exist in multiple states simultaneously thanks to superposition. This allows quantum machines to perform complex calculations at speeds unattainable by classical computers. For AI, this means:

- **Accelerated Machine Learning**: Training machine learning models, which traditionally requires significant time and computational resources, could be completed in a fraction of the time.

- **Enhanced Optimization**: Quantum algorithms can solve optimization problems more efficiently, benefiting AI tasks like route planning and resource allocation.

Transforming Data Processing

AI systems thrive on data. The ability of quantum computers to handle vast datasets more effectively could revolutionize various domains:

- **Big Data Analytics**: Quantum computing can process and analyze large volumes of data much faster than classical systems, leading to more accurate insights and predictions.

- **Complex Simulations**: Industries such as pharmaceuticals and materials science rely on simulations for research and development. Quantum-enhanced simulations can expedite these processes, leading to quicker innovations.

Real-World Applications

Several real-world applications illustrate the potential impact of quantum computing on AI:

Drug Discovery

Traditional drug discovery involves testing numerous compounds to identify potential candidates. Quantum computing can simulate molecular interactions at unprecedented speeds, enabling researchers to pinpoint viable drugs faster and with greater accuracy. This accelerates the development of new treatments and reduces costs.

Financial Modeling

Financial markets are intricate systems influenced by countless variables. Quantum algorithms can analyze these variables simultaneously, providing more precise risk assessments and optimized trading strategies. This has profound implications for investment firms seeking to maximize returns while minimizing risks.

Pioneering Research and Development

Leading technology companies are already exploring the synergy between quantum computing and AI. For instance:

- **Google's Quantum AI Lab**: Focuses on developing quantum algorithms for machine learning tasks.

- **IBM's Qiskit**: Provides tools for researchers to experiment with quantum-enhanced AI applications.

Challenges Ahead

Despite its promise, integrating quantum computing into mainstream AI applications faces several challenges:

- **Error Rates**: Quantum computers are prone to errors due to decoherence and noise, necessitating robust error-correction techniques.

- **Scalability**: Building scalable quantum systems that outperform classical counterparts remains a formidable challenge.

- **Accessibility**: Current quantum hardware is expensive and requires specialized knowledge, limiting widespread adoption.

Future Prospects

As research progresses, breakthroughs in these areas will pave the way for practical applications. Hypothetically speaking, envisioning a future where quantum-powered AI systems make real-time decisions in autonomous vehicles or manage global supply chains is not far-fetched.

Imagine an AI system analyzing all traffic data instantaneously, recalculating optimal routes dynamically through a city grid teeming with autonomous vehicles—this is the potential unlocked by combining AI with quantum computing.

The journey towards this reality involves navigating technical hurdles and fostering interdisciplinary collaboration. The interplay between these two cutting-edge technologies holds immense promise for exponential growth across sectors.

Timeline for Quantum Computing: How Far Are We?

Quantum computing is on the verge of transforming our technological landscape, with the potential to revolutionize various industries through its unmatched processing power. The journey towards fully functional quantum computers has been marked by significant milestones and formidable challenges. Understanding this timeline helps us grasp how far we've come and what lies ahead.

Early Developments: Laying the Groundwork

The origins of quantum computing can be traced back to the early 1980s when physicists like Richard Feynman and David Deutsch began exploring the possibilities of using quantum mechanics for computation. They proposed that certain problems that classical computers couldn't solve might be approached by leveraging quantum phenomena such as superposition and entanglement.

Key Milestones:

- *1981*: Richard Feynman proposes the concept of a quantum computer.

- *1994*: Peter Shor develops Shor's algorithm, demonstrating that a quantum computer could efficiently solve integer factorization, a problem critical for cryptography.

The Birth of Quantum Hardware

In the late 1990s and early 2000s, researchers started building basic quantum bits or qubits. These qubits are the fundamental units of quantum information, similar to bits in classical computing but with the ability to exist in multiple states at once.

Progress Highlights:

- *1998*: First experimental demonstration of quantum algorithms using nuclear magnetic resonance (NMR) techniques.

- *2001*: IBM constructs a 7-qubit quantum computer that successfully implements Shor's algorithm.

Rapid Progress: Entering the Quantum Race

Since then, companies, universities, and governments have invested heavily in creating scalable quantum systems. In the mid-2010s, major tech companies like Google, IBM, and Intel intensified their efforts, each announcing significant breakthroughs.

Notable Achievements:

- *2016*: IBM launches the IBM Q Experience, providing cloud-based access to a 5-qubit quantum processor.

- *2019*: Google claims "quantum supremacy" with its Sycamore processor performing a specific task faster than any existing classical supercomputer.

Current State: Bridging Theory and Practicality

Quantum computing has moved from theoretical concepts to working prototypes. However, these machines are still in their early stages compared to classical supercomputers. Issues such as how long qubits can maintain their state (coherence times) and error rates need to be addressed before practical applications become widespread.

Recent Developments:

- *2021*: IBM unveils its Eagle processor with 127 qubits, pushing the boundaries of qubit scalability.

- Ongoing research focuses on error correction techniques and building fault-tolerant quantum computers essential for reliable computations.

Future Prospects: Overcoming Challenges Ahead

The way forward involves overcoming technical obstacles while increasing the number of qubits without sacrificing stability. Quantum error correction remains one of the most critical areas requiring innovation since even small errors can lead to incorrect results in complex calculations.

Anticipated Breakthroughs:

- Development of **topological qubits**, which promise greater stability by encoding information in global properties resistant to local disturbances.

- Advancements in **quantum error correction codes**, necessary for maintaining data integrity over prolonged operations.

Strategic Roadmaps: Industry Forecasts

Tech companies have outlined ambitious plans predicting when we might see practical quantum computers making meaningful impacts on industries like pharmaceuticals, materials science, cryptography, and artificial intelligence.

Industry Predictions:

- **IBM's Quantum Roadmap** envisions building systems with thousands of qubits by 2023.

- **Google's Quantum AI Lab** aims for commercially viable quantum computers within this decade.

Exploring these timelines reveals a rapidly advancing field balancing between theoretical potential and practical realization. Each milestone brings us closer to unlocking new computational paradigms poised to redefine our technological capabilities.

Ethical Considerations in AI: Privacy, Bias, and Decision-Making

The rapid development of AI technology brings with it a host of ethical considerations that demand scrutiny. As AI systems become more integrated into everyday life, questions around privacy, bias, and decision-making grow increasingly urgent.

Privacy Concerns

AI's capability to process vast amounts of data can encroach on personal privacy.

Data Collection

AI systems, particularly those used in social media and online services, collect extensive user data. This data is often analyzed to create detailed profiles for targeted advertising or personalized experiences. The risk lies in the potential misuse or unauthorized access to this sensitive information.

Surveillance

Government and corporate surveillance powered by AI technologies can lead to invasions of privacy. Facial recognition software, for instance, raises alarms about constant monitoring and the erosion of anonymity in public spaces.

> **Example:** The controversy surrounding the use of facial recognition technology by law enforcement agencies highlights the balance between security and privacy. Critics argue that such technologies can infringe on civil liberties if not carefully regulated.

Bias in AI Systems

AI algorithms are only as unbiased as the data they are trained on. This leads to significant concerns regarding fairness and equality.

Training Data

If the data used to train an AI system reflects historical biases, the system will learn and perpetuate these biases. For instance, an AI hiring tool trained on resumes from a predominantly male workforce may favor male candidates.

Algorithmic Decisions

Biases in AI can manifest in various sectors including finance, healthcare, and criminal justice. These biases can result in unfair treatment of certain groups based on race, gender, or socioeconomic status.

> **Real-World Scenario:** A study by MIT Media Lab found that facial analysis algorithms had higher error rates for darker-skinned individuals compared to

lighter-skinned individuals. Such disparities under-score the need for diverse training datasets and inclu-sive algorithm development.

Decision-Making Transparency

AI systems often operate as "black boxes," making decisions without providing clear explanations. This opacity poses challenges for accountability and trust.

Explainability

Understanding how an AI system arrives at a decision is crucial for verifying its accuracy and fairness. Lack of transparency can lead to mistrust among users and stakeholders.

Accountability

When an AI system makes a mistake, it is essential to identify who is responsible—whether it's the developers, operators, or the technology itself. Clear accountability frameworks are necessary to address errors effectively.

> **Quote:** "AI should not be a black box; we must know how decisions are being made." - Tim Cook

Ethical Frameworks

Developing ethical frameworks for AI involves interdisciplinary collaboration among technologists, ethicists, policymakers, and the public.

Regulatory Standards

Governments worldwide are beginning to draft regulations aimed at ensuring ethical AI use. The European Union's General Data Protection Regulation (GDPR) sets stringent guidelines on data protection and privacy.

Corporate Responsibility

Companies developing AI technologies must adopt ethical guidelines that prioritize transparency, fairness, and accountability. Initiatives such as Google's AI Principles emphasize responsible innovation.

Moving Forward

Addressing ethical considerations in AI requires ongoing dialogue and adaptive strategies. Engaging diverse perspectives ensures that ethical frameworks evolve alongside technological advancements.

> **Metaphor:** Just as a compass guides explorers through uncharted territories, robust ethical guidelines steer the development and deployment of AI towards a future that benefits all of humanity.

Ethical considerations form the bedrock upon which trust in AI is built. By tackling issues related to privacy, bias, and decision-making head-on, society can harness AI's potential while safeguarding fundamental human rights.

Economic Impact of AI: Job Displacement and Creation

Artificial Intelligence (AI) is starting to change the economy, causing significant changes in job markets around the world. As AI technologies improve, their effects on jobs become more complicated. The balance between job loss and job creation is an important area of interest.

Job Displacement: The Inevitable Consequence

AI's ability to automate tasks previously performed by humans leads to a palpable sense of unease among workers. According to a study by McKinsey Global Institute, up to 800 million jobs could be lost worldwide to automation by 2030. This potential displacement spans various sectors:

- **Manufacturing**: Robotics and AI-driven machinery streamline production processes, reducing the need for manual labor.

- **Retail**: Automated checkout systems and inventory management tools diminish the demand for cashiers and stock clerks.

- **Customer Service**: Chatbots and virtual assistants handle basic customer inquiries, replacing entry-level customer service roles.

While these changes can lead to improved efficiency and cost savings for businesses, they pose a significant threat to workers reliant on these jobs. A vivid example is the automobile industry, where assembly lines now employ robotic arms for precision tasks, displacing human workers who once performed these functions.

Job Creation: New Opportunities Arise

Conversely, AI also generates new employment opportunities. Emerging roles often require specialized skills in AI development, maintenance, and application. Key areas include:

- **Data Science**: Professionals skilled in data analysis and machine learning algorithms are in high demand.

- **AI Ethics**: The rise of ethical considerations surrounding AI use necessitates experts who can navigate these complex issues.

- **Maintenance and Support**: As AI systems proliferate, so does the need for technicians who can ensure their optimal functioning.

A poignant illustration is the tech industry itself. Companies like Google and Amazon have expanded their workforces significantly as they develop and integrate AI technologies into their operations.

Sector-Specific Impacts

The economic effects of AI vary across different sectors:

- **Healthcare**: While AI streamlines diagnostics and treatment plans, it also creates jobs in health informatics and telemedicine.

- **Finance**: Algorithmic trading and risk management systems reduce the need for certain roles but boost demand for financial technology experts.

- **Education**: Personalized learning platforms may replace traditional teaching methods but open up avenues for educational content creation and platform management.

These sector-specific impacts underscore the necessity for adaptability within the workforce. Workers must pivot towards acquiring new skills that align with emerging job opportunities.

The Role of Education and Training

Educational institutions play a crucial role in preparing individuals for an AI-driven economy. Emphasis on STEM (Science, Technology, Engineering, Mathematics) education is paramount. Vocational training programs tailored to future job markets can also bridge skill gaps.

Governments and private enterprises should invest in reskilling initiatives to facilitate smooth transitions for displaced workers:

> "The best way to predict your future is to create it." –
> Abraham Lincoln

This quote encapsulates the proactive stance required from both individuals and organizations in navigating the economic impact of AI.

Balancing Act: Policy Interventions

Policymakers face the challenge of balancing job displacement with job creation. Implementing measures such as:

1. **Universal Basic Income (UBI)**: Providing financial security as people transition between jobs.

2. **Tax Incentives**: Encouraging companies to invest in human capital development alongside technological advancements.

These interventions aim to mitigate adverse effects while fostering a conducive environment for innovation.

AI's dual role in displacing certain jobs while creating new ones underscores its transformative power within economies. Understanding this dynamic is key to leveraging AI's benefits while addressing its challenges effectively.

Social Implications of AI: Changes in Daily Life

Artificial Intelligence (AI) has become an integral part of our daily lives, subtly changing the way we live, work, and interact. From self-operating home devices to customized online experiences, AI's impact is everywhere and significant.

Enhanced Convenience and Efficiency

AI-powered technologies make everyday tasks easier and more efficient:

- **Smart Home Devices**: Voice-activated assistants like Amazon Alexa and Google Home can do everything from setting reminders to controlling appliances. Picture this: you wake up to an AI-designed morning routine where your coffee is brewed, thermostat adjusted, and news headlines read aloud.

- **Personalized Recommendations**: Streaming platforms such as Netflix and Spotify use AI algorithms to recommend content based on individual preferences. This personalization improves user experience by minimizing the time spent searching for entertainment.

Transforming Communication

AI has also completely changed the way we communicate with others:

- **Chatbots and Virtual Assistants**: Companies use AI-powered chatbots on their websites and social media pages to provide immediate customer support. These virtual helpers efficiently handle questions, ensuring 24/7 service without human involvement.

- **Language Translation**: Apps like Google Translate employ machine learning to overcome language barriers instantly. This feature promotes global communication, allowing individuals from different language backgrounds to connect effortlessly.

Healthcare Innovations

AI's influence goes beyond convenience into critical fields like healthcare:

- **Telemedicine**: With AI-powered diagnostic tools, doctors can offer accurate consultations remotely. This advancement is especially beneficial in rural or underserved regions where access to healthcare facilities is limited.

- **Wearable Health Monitors**: Gadgets like Fitbit and Apple Watch use AI algorithms to monitor vital signs and predict potential health problems. Users receive personalized health insights, empowering them to make informed lifestyle choices.

Ethical Considerations

Even with its advantages, AI raises important ethical issues that need attention:

- **Privacy Issues**: The extensive data collection required for AI functionality poses risks to individual privacy. Concerns arise about how personal information is stored, used, and safeguarded against breaches.

- **Bias and Fairness**: AI systems can unintentionally reinforce biases present in training data. For instance, facial recognition technologies have shown higher error rates in identifying individuals from certain demographic groups. Tackling these biases is essential for ensuring fair outcomes.

Employment Shifts

The integration of AI into various industries has sparked discussions about its effect on jobs:

- **Job Displacement**: Automation of repetitive tasks threatens jobs traditionally performed by humans. Industries such as manufacturing and retail are experiencing changes as machines take over manual labor roles.

- **New Job Creation**: On the flip side, AI also creates new job opportunities in tech development, data analysis, and cybersecurity. The evolving job market requires reskilling programs to prepare workers for emerging roles.

Social Interaction Evolution

AI influences not only professional but also personal relationships:

- **Social Media Algorithms**: Platforms like Facebook and Instagram utilize AI to curate content feeds based on user behavior. While this personalization boosts engagement, it can also create echo chambers that limit exposure to diverse viewpoints.

- **Virtual Companions**: Applications powered by AI like Replika provide companionship through conversational agents designed to imitate human interaction. These virtual friends offer emotional support but raise concerns about the authenticity of genuine human connection.

The social implications of AI are complex, affecting various aspects of daily life. From improving convenience and communication to raising ethical dilemmas and reshaping employment landscapes, AI's impact is both transformative and intricate. As we navigate these changes, ongoing discussions around ethical practices and societal effects will be crucial for responsibly harnessing the full potential of artificial intelligence.

Preparing for an AI-Driven Future: Skills and Adaptability

The rapid advancement of AI technology is reshaping the job landscape, prompting professionals to develop new skills and adapt to an evolving work environment. As industries integrate AI into their operations, understanding which skills are becoming essential and how to cultivate adaptability is crucial.

The Imperative of Lifelong Learning

Adopting a mindset of lifelong learning has never been more critical. Professionals must continuously update their knowledge base to keep pace with technological advancements.

Technical Skills

Proficiency in programming languages such as Python, R, and Java is invaluable. Familiarity with machine learning frameworks like TensorFlow and PyTorch can differentiate candidates in the job market.

Data Literacy

Understanding data analytics, data visualization, and basic statistics is foundational. These skills enable individuals to interpret data-driven insights effectively.

AI Ethics and Governance

Awareness of the ethical implications of AI applications ensures responsible use. Knowledge of regulatory standards and best practices helps mitigate risks associated with AI deployment.

Soft Skills: The Human Touch

While technical prowess is essential, soft skills remain irreplaceable by machines. These skills enhance professional effectiveness and foster a collaborative work environment.

Emotional Intelligence

The ability to recognize, understand, and manage emotions enhances interpersonal relationships. It is crucial for leadership roles where empathy and communication are key.

Critical Thinking

Analyzing situations logically and making informed decisions are vital in navigating complex problems that AI solutions may present.

Creativity

Innovation drives progress. Creative thinking leads to unique solutions that may not be within the purview of algorithmic approaches.

Adaptability in the Face of Change

Adaptability encompasses both a willingness to embrace change and the capability to thrive in new circumstances. It involves:

- **Agility**: The ability to pivot quickly in response to new information or changes in the external environment. Agile methodologies often applied in software development can extend to broader organizational practices.

- **Resilience**: Building mental resilience allows individuals to cope with setbacks and stress associated with rapid technological shifts.

- **Continuous Improvement**: Embracing a culture of continuous improvement encourages regular skill enhancement and process optimization.

Building Interdisciplinary Knowledge

Interdisciplinary knowledge combines insights from various fields, fostering innovation at the intersections of different domains.

- **Cross-functional Expertise**: Combining knowledge from fields such as business management, cognitive psychology, and computer science can lead to holistic AI solutions.

- **Collaboration Across Disciplines**: Working closely with professionals from diverse backgrounds sparks creativity and broadens perspectives on problem-solving.

Upskilling Resources

Numerous resources are available for those seeking to enhance their skill sets:

- **Online Courses**: Platforms like Coursera, edX, and Udacity offer courses on AI, machine learning, data science, and related fields.

- **Workshops and Bootcamps**: Intensive training sessions provide hands-on experience with real-world projects.

- **Professional Certifications**: Certifications from recognized institutions validate expertise in specific areas such as data analysis or project management.

Embracing lifelong learning, honing soft skills, developing adaptability, building interdisciplinary knowledge, leveraging upskilling resources—all these efforts position individuals favorably in an AI-driven future. The objective is not merely survival but thriving amidst technological transformation.

At Risk Careers and Vocations

Data Entry and Clerical Work

Data entry tasks are essential for many administrative functions in organizations. These tasks usually involve entering, updating, and managing data into systems like databases, spreadsheets, or specialized software. Because data entry is routine, it can easily be automated using artificial intelligence (AI) technologies.

Overview of Data Entry Tasks

Data entry includes various activities:

- **Inputting data**: Manually typing information from paper documents or digital sources into electronic formats.

- **Updating records**: Regularly modifying existing entries to ensure accuracy.

- **Data verification**: Checking for errors and inconsistencies within datasets.

- **Database management**: Organizing and maintaining large volumes of data for easy retrieval.

These tasks are often repetitive and time-consuming, making them ideal candidates for automation.

Automation Potential in Clerical Roles

There is a huge potential for automation in clerical roles. AI-powered tools can perform these tasks more efficiently, accurately, and at a much lower cost than human labor. Moving towards AI-driven solutions can lead to significant improvements in productivity and fewer mistakes.

Several factors highlight this potential:

1. **Consistency and Accuracy**: AI systems eliminate human errors that occur due to fatigue or oversight.

2. **Speed**: Automated processes handle large volumes of data significantly faster than manual methods.

3. **Cost-effectiveness**: Reducing the need for extensive human intervention decreases operational costs.

These benefits explain why many companies are heavily investing in AI technologies to automate clerical work.

Examples of AI Tools That Streamline Data Entry Processes

Various AI tools have emerged to streamline data entry processes:

- **Optical Character Recognition (OCR)**: OCR technology converts different types of documents, such as scanned paper documents or PDFs, into editable and searchable data. Tools like Adobe Acrobat DC utilize OCR for efficient data extraction.

- **Robotic Process Automation (RPA)**: RPA platforms like UiPath and Blue Prism automate repetitive tasks by mimicking human actions interacting with digital systems. These tools can be programmed to handle tasks such as invoice processing and report generation.

- **Natural Language Processing (NLP)**: NLP tools process unstructured text data. For example, IBM Watson uses NLP to analyze text-based information, extracting relevant data points automatically.

- **Machine Learning Algorithms**: Machine learning models can predict and fill in missing information based on historical data trends. An example is Google's AutoML, which simplifies the creation of custom machine learning models tailored to specific needs.

These tools show the significant progress AI has made in automating clerical work.

Real-world Example

Consider the case study of a multinational corporation that implemented RPA to manage its invoice processing system. Prior to automation, a team of clerks manually inputted thousands of invoices monthly—a task fraught with delays and errors. Post-implementation, the company saw a 60% reduction in processing time and a dramatic decrease in errors, showcasing the transformative power of AI in clerical roles.

Shifting focus from conventional methods to AI-driven processes not only enhances efficiency but also liberates human workers from monotonous tasks. This allows them to engage in more strategic activities that require creativity and critical thinking—attributes where humans continue to outshine machines.

The path towards increased automation in clerical jobs is clear. As businesses strive for greater efficiency and reduced operational costs, embracing AI becomes imperative. This evolution signals a paradigm shift where humans work alongside intelligent systems rather than being replaced outright, creating a balanced dynamic between technology's capabilities and human ingenuity.

Customer Service and Support

Impact of AI on Customer Service Roles

Artificial intelligence (AI) has significantly reshaped the landscape of customer service roles. Traditional customer service tasks, which often involve repetitive inquiries and standard responses, are being increasingly managed by AI-driven chatbots and virtual assistants. These technologies can handle a high volume of queries simultaneously, ensuring that customers receive prompt and accurate information.

Benefits of AI in Customer Service

1. **Efficiency**: AI systems streamline the customer service process, reducing wait times and improving response accuracy. This efficiency not only enhances customer satisfaction but also allows human agents to focus on more complex issues that require a personal touch.

2. **Cost Reduction**: By automating routine tasks, companies can reduce operational costs associated with hiring and training large customer support teams.

3. **24/7 Availability**: Unlike human agents, AI systems can operate around the clock, providing constant support to customers across different time zones.

A clear example of this transformation is seen in the banking sector. Banks increasingly use AI to manage customer inquiries about account balances, transaction histories, and loan applications. This has led to a significant reduction in the need for extensive call center staff.

Evolution of Support Systems Through AI

Support systems have evolved from simple automated voice response units to sophisticated AI-driven platforms capable of understanding and processing natural language.

Key Technologies Driving This Evolution

- **Natural Language Processing (NLP)**: AI systems now employ NLP to understand and respond to customer queries in a conversational manner. This technology enables chatbots to process complex sentences and provide relevant answers.

- **Machine Learning**: Machine learning algorithms continuously improve the performance of AI systems by learning from past interactions. Over time, these systems become more adept at handling a wide variety of customer inquiries.

- **Omnichannel Support**: Modern AI solutions integrate seamlessly with various communication channels such as email, social media, and live chat. This ensures a consistent customer experience regardless of the platform used.

For instance, e-commerce giants like Amazon leverage AI-driven chatbots to handle common inquiries about order status, returns, and product information across multiple platforms. This integration facilitates a smoother shopping experience for customers while optimizing operational efficiency for the company.

Case Studies of Successful AI Implementations in Customer Service

Several organizations have successfully implemented AI solutions in their customer service operations, leading to notable improvements in both efficiency and customer satisfaction.

1. **Sephora**:

- *Virtual Artist*: Sephora's Virtual Artist uses augmented reality powered by AI to help customers try on makeup products digitally before making a purchase. This tool provides personalized recommendations based on individual preferences.

- *AI Chatbots*: Sephora employs chatbots to assist customers with product inquiries and appointment bookings through messaging apps like Facebook Messenger.

1. **H&M**:

- *Customer Support Chatbot*: H&M's chatbot guides customers through product selections based on their style preferences. It also assists with order tracking and return processes.

- *Personalized Shopping Experience*: The chatbot collects data from interactions to offer tailored fashion advice and product suggestions.

1. **Lemonade Insurance**:

- *Claims Processing*: Lemonade utilizes an AI bot named "Jim" for claims processing. Jim can handle claims within seconds by analyzing policy details and assessing damage through uploaded photos or videos.

- *Customer Onboarding*: Their onboarding bot "Maya" helps new customers understand policies, get quotes, and sign up for insurance plans effortlessly.

These case studies demonstrate how businesses across various industries are harnessing the power of AI to transform their customer service operations. By adopting advanced technologies like chatbots and virtual assistants, companies not only enhance their service delivery but also gain valuable insights into consumer behavior patterns.

In essence, the integration of AI into customer service roles represents a paradigm shift towards more efficient, cost-effective, and personalized support systems. This evolution underscores the potential for significant job displacement in traditional roles while simultaneously creating opportunities for new skill sets centered around managing and optimizing these intelligent systems.

Basic Manufacturing and Assembly Line Jobs

Overview of Manufacturing Tasks Prone to Automation

Manufacturing jobs have long been the backbone of industrial economies. However, these roles are increasingly susceptible to automation due to their repetitive and predictable nature. Tasks such as:

- **Material handling**

- **Quality control inspections**

- **Packaging and labeling**

- **Assembly of components**

are prime candidates for automation. These activities often require limited human judgment and can be replicated by machines with a high degree of accuracy.

The Role of Robotics in Replacing Manual Labor

Robotics has revolutionized the manufacturing sector by minimizing human error and enhancing efficiency. Consider the assembly line—a hallmark of mass production since Henry Ford's era. Today, robotic arms equipped with advanced sensors and machine learning algorithms perform tasks that once required manual labor:

- **Welding robots**: Used extensively in automotive manufacturing to ensure precision and speed.

- **Pick-and-place robots**: Capable of picking up items from one location and placing them in another with remarkable accuracy.

- **Inspection robots**: Utilizing computer vision to detect defects far more accurately than the human eye.

Industrial robot adoption is not merely about replacing human workers; it's about enhancing capabilities. A welding robot can work around the clock without fatigue, ensuring consistent quality and throughput.

Future Trends in Automated Manufacturing

The landscape of automated manufacturing is continuously evolving, driven by advancements in artificial intelligence, machine learning, and IoT (Internet of Things). Key trends shaping the future include:

1. Collaborative Robots (Cobots)

Designed to work alongside humans, cobots are equipped with safety features that allow them to operate in close proximity to people without causing harm. They are already making significant inroads into small and medium-sized enterprises (SMEs) by handling tasks such as assembly, painting, and packaging.

2. Smart Factories

The concept of smart factories leverages IoT devices to create an interconnected network where machines communicate with each other. This connectivity allows for real-time monitoring and optimization of production processes, reducing downtime and increasing efficiency.

3. Additive Manufacturing (3D Printing)

Unlike traditional subtractive manufacturing methods that remove material to create objects, additive manufacturing builds products layer by layer. This technology not only reduces waste but also allows for complex designs that are impossible or cost-prohibitive with conventional techniques.

4. Predictive Maintenance

AI-driven predictive maintenance systems analyze data from machinery to predict failures before they occur. This proactive approach reduces downtime and extends the lifespan of equipment.

5. AI-Powered Quality Control

Advanced AI algorithms are being used for real-time quality control by analyzing images or sensor data to detect defects during the production process. This ensures higher product quality and reduces waste.

Industry leaders like Tesla have already embraced these technologies, creating highly automated manufacturing environments where human intervention is minimal but essential for oversight and innovation.

> "Automation applied to an inefficient operation will
> magnify the inefficiency." — Bill Gates

The integration of robotics into manufacturing is not a panacea but a tool for achieving greater efficiency when applied correctly. The shift towards automation necessitates a reevaluation of workforce skills, emphasizing the need for continuous learning and adaptation.

By understanding these evolving trends, organizations can better prepare for a future where human ingenuity complements robotic precision, creating a harmonious blend that drives unprecedented productivity in manufacturing sectors globally.

Retail Sales and Cashier Positions

Retail jobs and **cashier positions** have been essential components of the commercial landscape for decades. Yet, with the advent of AI technologies, these roles are undergoing significant transformations that promise to reshape the industry.

Changes in Retail Due to AI-Driven Checkouts

AI-driven checkouts represent a paradigm shift in how retail transactions are conducted. Traditional checkout processes often involve long lines and manual scanning of items by cashiers. Here, AI steps in to create a seamless experience:

1. **Self-checkout Kiosks**: These systems allow customers to scan and bag their items independently, reducing the need for human cashiers.

2. **Smart Carts**: Equipped with sensors and cameras, smart carts automatically detect and register items as they are placed inside, allowing customers to bypass traditional checkouts entirely.

3. **Amazon Go Stores**: Utilizing advanced computer vision and sensor fusion technologies, these stores enable a "just walk out" shopping experience where customers simply leave with their products, and the payment is processed automatically.

The transformation brought about by AI-driven checkouts addresses several pain points associated with traditional retail experiences, offering speed, convenience, and efficiency.

The Role of Virtual Assistants in Enhancing Customer Experience

Virtual assistants are becoming integral to enhancing customer interactions within retail environments. These AI-driven tools provide personalized assistance that rivals—and sometimes surpasses—that offered by human staff:

- **Chatbots**: Deployed on websites and mobile apps, chatbots assist customers with queries, product recommendations, and troubleshooting issues. They operate 24/7 with consistent accuracy.

- **Voice Assistants**: Devices like Amazon's Alexa or Google Home facilitate hands-free shopping experiences. Customers can inquire about product details or place orders using simple voice commands.

- **In-store Assistance**: Robots such as LoweBot in Lowe's stores guide customers to desired products while providing information about stock availability.

Virtual assistants streamline the customer journey from discovery to purchase, significantly enhancing user satisfaction.

Job Implications for Cashiers and Retail Staff

The adoption of AI technologies in retail raises important questions regarding job implications for cashiers and other retail staff. While automation offers numerous benefits to businesses and consumers alike, it inevitably impacts the workforce:

1. **Job Displacement**: The most immediate effect is a reduction in demand for traditional cashier roles as self-checkout systems and smart carts become more prevalent.

2. **Skill Shift**: As routine tasks become automated, there is a growing need for employees who possess technical skills to manage and maintain these AI systems.

3. **Enhanced Roles**: Rather than eliminating positions altogether, some retailers are reimagining roles where staff focus on customer service excellence rather than transactional duties.

Retailers like Walmart have implemented initiatives to retrain staff for higher-skilled positions within their organizations. This transition underscores the importance of adaptability in a tech-driven workplace.

The integration of AI into retail environments reflects an ongoing evolution that promises both challenges and opportunities. Retail professionals must navigate this landscape by embracing new technologies while cultivating skills that complement automated processes.

By examining how AI transforms retail sales and cashier positions, we gain insight into broader trends affecting various sectors—a testament to the disruptive power of technology in reshaping industries worldwide.

Routine Administrative Tasks

Administrative tasks are the backbone of any organization, often perceived as mundane yet indispensable. These routine activities are increasingly susceptible to **AI replacement** due to their repetitive and rule-based nature.

Common Administrative Tasks Susceptible to AI Replacement

Routine administrative work includes a variety of tasks that can be efficiently handled by AI:

- **Scheduling Meetings:** Coordinating calendars, setting up meetings, and sending reminders.

- **Data Entry:** Inputting data into spreadsheets or databases.

- **Email Management:** Sorting, prioritizing, and responding to emails.

- **Document Preparation:** Drafting standard documents, proofreading, and formatting.

- **Travel Arrangements:** Booking flights, hotels, and transportation.

Each of these tasks demands precision but lacks the necessity for human intuition or creativity. AI systems excel in such environments where rules are clear and exceptions are minimal.

Tools That Automate Scheduling and Communications

The rise of AI-driven tools has revolutionized how businesses handle administrative functions. Consider these examples:

1. **Calendly**: This tool automates meeting scheduling by allowing individuals to set their availability and preferences. It integrates with various calendar systems to ensure seamless coordination without the need for endless email exchanges.

2. **Grammarly**: Beyond just a spell checker, Grammarly uses AI to suggest improvements in grammar, tone, and style for document preparation. It ensures that communications maintain professionalism and clarity.

3. **X.AI**: An AI assistant specifically designed for scheduling meetings. Users can CC the assistant in emails, and it will automatically manage the back-and-forth communication required to find suitable times for all parties involved.

4. **Zoho Mail's Zia**: An intelligent email assistant that categorizes emails, prioritizes important messages, and can even draft responses based on past interactions.

The Future of Administrative Roles in a Tech-Driven Workplace

As AI continues to advance, the landscape of administrative roles is poised for significant transformation:

- **Focus on Strategic Tasks**: With routine tasks automated, administrative professionals can shift their focus towards more strategic responsibilities like project management, process optimization, and team coordination.

- **Skill Evolution**: The demand for skills will evolve from basic clerical abilities to proficiency in managing AI tools, interpreting data insights generated by these systems, and making informed decisions based on this data.

- **Hybrid Roles**: New hybrid roles may emerge where administrative duties are combined with IT support functions. Professionals in these roles would ensure smooth operation of AI tools while also handling traditional administrative tasks when needed.

AI's ability to handle routine work with high efficiency allows organizations to redirect human talent towards areas requiring emotional intelligence, creativity, and complex problem-solving—qualities currently beyond the reach of artificial intelligence.

The office environment itself may undergo changes as well. Open-plan offices optimized for collaboration might see an increase in quiet zones where employees focus on higher-order tasks without interruption from routine chores managed by AI assistants.

As we contemplate a tech-driven future workplace enriched by automation technologies like AI:

> *"Automation applied to an inefficient operation will magnify the inefficiency."* - Bill Gates

This quote underscores the importance of integrating AI thoughtfully within existing workflows. Organizations must refine their processes before leveraging automation technology; otherwise, they risk amplifying inefficiencies rather than mitigating them.

Ultimately, while routine administrative tasks are prime candidates for automation due to their repetitive nature, the future role of administrative professionals hinges on their adaptability and willingness to embrace new technologies. The shift promises not only greater efficiency but also enriched job satisfaction through engagement in more meaningful work.

Basic Financial Analysis and Accounting

AI advancements are transforming the world of financial analysis and accounting. Financial analysts and accountants, who used to spend a lot of time gathering data and crunching numbers, are now seeing their roles change as artificial intelligence reshapes the industry.

How AI Performs Basic Financial Analysis More Efficiently

AI-powered tools are great at doing basic financial analysis because they use machine learning algorithms and large amounts of data. These technologies **analyze past data**, find patterns, and predict future trends faster and more accurately than ever before. For example:

- **Predictive Analytics**: AI systems predict market trends based on past data, improving investment strategies.

- **Risk Assessment**: Machine learning models assess risk factors more accurately by looking at multiple variables at once.

These AI abilities not only speed up the analysis process but also minimize human mistakes, providing more trustworthy insights for decision-making.

Tools That Assist Accountants with Routine Tasks

Many AI-based tools have come out to make routine accounting tasks easier, such as:

1. **Automated Bookkeeping Software**: Tools like Quick-Books Online use AI to automatically categorize transactions, cutting down on manual data entry.

2. **Expense Management Systems**: Platforms like Expensify use OCR (Optical Character Recognition) to scan receipts and automate expense reporting.

3. **Reconciliation Software**: Solutions like Xero use AI to match bank transactions with accounting records, making

reconciliation processes easier.

By automating these repetitive tasks, accountants can concentrate on strategic activities like financial planning and advisory services, adding more value to their organizations.

Implications for the Accounting Profession Moving Forward

The integration of AI into financial analysis and accounting brings about significant changes for professionals in the field.

Shift in Skill Requirements

The need for traditional bookkeeping skills is decreasing while proficiency in data analysis and knowledge of AI tools is becoming essential.

Job Displacement vs. Job Evolution

While some routine jobs may disappear, new opportunities are arising in areas like forensic accounting, compliance management, and financial consulting.

Enhanced Decision-Making

Accountants using AI tools can offer deeper insights and more strategic advice, moving from a transactional role to a more consultative position within their organizations.

In simple terms, using AI in finance isn't just about replacing human jobs; it's also about redefining them. As technology keeps evolving, accountants will have to adapt by learning new skills that use the power of AI to provide greater value.

Transportation and Delivery Services

Overview of Transportation Roles at Risk from Automation

Transportation jobs have always been a cornerstone of the global economy, providing essential services in logistics, freight, and passenger conveyance. However, these roles are increasingly susceptible to automation due to advancements in AI and robotics. Key positions at risk include:

- **Truck Drivers**: Long-haul trucking is a prime candidate for automation. Autonomous trucks can operate continuously without the need for rest breaks, reducing transportation time and costs.

- **Taxi and Ride-Sharing Drivers**: Companies like Uber and Lyft are investing heavily in self-driving technologies to reduce reliance on human drivers.

- **Delivery Couriers**: With the rise of e-commerce, delivery services are under pressure to become more efficient. Autonomous delivery vehicles and drones present viable alternatives.

The Rise of Autonomous Delivery Systems

Autonomous delivery systems are not just a futuristic concept; they are becoming a reality. These systems encompass a variety of technologies designed to replace human labor in transporting goods from one location to another.

Types of Autonomous Delivery Systems:

- **Self-Driving Trucks**: Companies such as Tesla and Waymo are developing autonomous trucks capable of long-distance travel without human intervention.

- **Delivery Drones**: Amazon's Prime Air aims to deliver packages up to five pounds in 30 minutes or less using small drones.

- **Robotic Couriers**: Startups like Starship Technologies are deploying small, autonomous robots for last-mile deliveries.

Case Studies on Companies Implementing These Technologies

Several companies are already pioneering the use of autonomous technologies in transportation and delivery services, setting benchmarks for the industry.

Self-Driving Trucks:

One notable example is Waymo, Google's self-driving technology subsidiary. Waymo has been testing its autonomous trucks on highways across the United States. According to Waymo's internal data, their trucks have driven over 20 million miles autonomously on public roads by 2022.

> "We envision a future where road freight transportation is safer and more efficient through automation," states John Krafcik, CEO of Waymo.

Delivery Drones:

Amazon's Prime Air program is another groundbreaking initiative. In December 2016, Amazon made its first successful drone delivery in Cambridge, UK. Although regulatory hurdles remain, Amazon continues to push forward with its drone technology.

> "The goal is to get packages into customers' hands in 30 minutes or less," says Jeff Bezos, founder of Amazon.

Robotic Couriers:

Starship Technologies has deployed robotic couriers that can navigate sidewalks autonomously. These robots are equipped with cameras and sensors to avoid obstacles and ensure safe deliveries. They have been successfully tested in cities like Milton Keynes in the UK and Washington D.C. in the USA.

> "Our robots can deliver groceries, take-out food, or even parcels right to your doorstep," claims Ahti Heinla, co-founder of Starship Technologies.

Future Trends in Automated Transportation

As AI continues evolving, predicting future trends becomes crucial for understanding how transportation jobs will transform:

1. **Increased Adoption**: More companies will adopt autonomous vehicles as technology becomes more reliable and cost-effective.

2. **Regulatory Changes**: Governments will need to update regulations to ensure safety while encouraging innovation.

3. **Job Reallocation**: While some roles will be eliminated, new opportunities will emerge in vehicle maintenance, oversight roles, and tech development.

The landscape of transportation jobs is shifting dramatically through innovations that promise efficiency but also pose challenges for the workforce.

Simple Legal Research and Document Review

Impact of AI on Legal Research Efficiency

Legal research constitutes a significant portion of a lawyer's workload, demanding meticulous attention to detail and extensive hours sifting through case law, statutes, and regulations. *Artificial Intelligence (AI)* is revolutionizing this domain by dramatically enhancing efficiency. Algorithms equipped with natural language processing (NLP) capabilities can analyze and interpret vast amounts of legal texts at unprecedented speeds.

Key Benefits:

- **Speed:** AI can process thousands of documents in minutes, a task that would take human researchers weeks.

- **Accuracy:** Advanced algorithms reduce the risk of human error, ensuring that no critical precedent or statute is overlooked.

- **Cost-Efficiency:** By cutting down the time needed for research, firms can reduce billable hours and offer more competitive pricing to clients.

Tools Simplifying Document Review Processes

Document review is another area where AI has made significant inroads. Traditionally, this process involves manually combing through volumes of paperwork to identify relevant information, an endeavor prone to errors and inefficiencies.

Noteworthy AI Tools:

- **eBrevia:** Utilizing machine learning, eBrevia automates contract review processes, extracting key provisions and clauses with high precision.

- **Kira Systems:** Known for its ability to identify and analyze clauses in contracts, Kira Systems enhances due diligence efforts by flagging potential issues swiftly.

- **ROSS Intelligence:** Leveraging IBM's Watson, ROSS provides comprehensive legal research assistance by quickly pinpointing relevant case law and statutes.

These tools not only expedite the review process but also ensure higher accuracy, transforming how legal professionals approach document analysis.

Future Prospects for Paralegals and Legal Assistants

The rise of AI-driven solutions inevitably raises questions about the future role of paralegals and legal assistants. While some fear job displacement, a more nuanced perspective reveals opportunities for role evolution rather than outright replacement.

Anticipated Changes:

1. **Shift in Responsibilities:** Paralegals may transition from performing routine tasks to more complex analytical roles, focusing on strategy formulation rather than data gathering.

2. **Enhanced Skill Sets:** The demand for tech-savvy legal professionals will surge as familiarity with AI tools becomes essential. Upskilling in areas such as data analytics and software management will be crucial.

3. **Collaborative Roles:** Rather than replacing human workers, AI will likely augment their capabilities. Paralegals can

leverage AI for preliminary research while dedicating their expertise to nuanced tasks requiring human judgment.

"AI in legal services is not about replacing paralegals; it's about empowering them to deliver more value by focusing on substantive work," says John Fernandez, Chief Innovation Officer at Dentons.

This synergy between technology and human expertise underscores the evolving landscape of legal professions. The integration of AI in legal research and document review exemplifies a broader trend where automation handles repetitive tasks, allowing professionals to concentrate on higher-order thinking and client interactions.

The transformative power of AI in the legal field cannot be overstated. Its ability to speed up processes while maintaining accuracy reshapes traditional workflows. This shift invites both excitement and caution as the industry navigates these groundbreaking changes.

Radiology and Basic Medical Diagnostics

Role of AI in Medical Imaging Interpretation

Artificial Intelligence (AI) has become an indispensable player in the realm of medical diagnostics, particularly in radiology. Traditional methods of diagnosing diseases through imaging required highly skilled radiologists to meticulously analyze X-rays, MRIs, and CT scans. AI algorithms now complement this expertise by offering enhanced precision and efficiency. These algorithms can identify patterns and abnormalities in imaging data with remarkable accuracy, often surpassing human capabilities.

How AI is Transforming Medical Imaging

- **Deep Learning Models**: AI employs deep learning models trained on vast datasets of medical images. This enables the technology to recognize complex patterns and subtle differences that might elude even seasoned professionals.

- **Real-Time Analysis**: AI systems provide real-time analysis, significantly reducing the time taken for diagnosis. This is crucial in emergency situations where timely intervention can be life-saving.

- **Error Reduction**: Human error is an inevitable part of manual diagnostic processes. AI minimizes these errors by offering consistent and reliable interpretations.

Benefits of Automating Diagnostic Processes

Automating diagnostic processes through AI offers a plethora of benefits to healthcare providers, patients, and the overall medical infrastructure.

1. Efficiency and Speed

AI-powered diagnostic tools streamline workflows, enabling faster patient turnover without compromising the quality of care. For instance, automated image analysis can flag critical cases immediately, ensuring prompt attention from medical professionals.

2. Cost Reduction

Automation reduces the cost associated with labor-intensive diagnostic procedures. Healthcare facilities can reallocate resources to other critical areas, optimizing operational budgets.

3. Enhanced Accuracy

AI systems are capable of analyzing vast amounts of data quickly and accurately. This leads to better diagnostic outcomes as potential issues are identified early on. For example:

- **Cancer Detection**: AI has shown proficiency in detecting various forms of cancer at early stages through imaging techniques.

- **Cardiovascular Issues**: Algorithms can analyze heart scans to detect irregularities that might indicate underlying cardiovascular conditions.

Future Implications for Radiologists in Healthcare Settings

The integration of AI in radiology does not spell the end for radiologists but rather transforms their roles within healthcare settings.

Augmentation Rather Than Replacement

Radiologists will increasingly collaborate with AI systems to enhance their diagnostic capabilities. The role shifts from primary diagnostician to an expert who interprets AI-generated insights, providing a more comprehensive evaluation.

Continuous Learning and Adaptation

AI's presence necessitates continuous learning for healthcare professionals. Radiologists must stay updated with technological advancements, understanding how to leverage these tools effectively.

> "AI will not replace radiologists, but radiologists who use AI will replace those who don't." - Dr. Curtis Langlotz

Ethical Considerations

The ethical implications surrounding the deployment of AI in medical diagnostics cannot be ignored. Radiologists will play a pivotal role in addressing these concerns:

- **Patient Privacy**: Ensuring that patient data used for training AI models is anonymized and securely stored.

- **Bias Mitigation**: Working towards eliminating biases that may exist within algorithmic decision-making processes to provide equitable care across diverse populations.

Job Market Dynamics

The demand for radiologists may shift geographically as rural or underserved areas benefit from tele-radiology services powered by AI.

Radiology jobs will evolve significantly as automation becomes more prevalent. While some routine tasks may be automated, the critical thinking and nuanced judgment provided by human experts remain irreplaceable.

Telemarketing and Sales Calls

How Telemarketing is Evolving with AI Solutions

Telemarketing has long been a cornerstone of direct marketing strategies, connecting businesses with potential customers through outbound calls. However, the landscape of telemarketing jobs is rapidly changing due to advancements in AI technologies. Traditional call centers are now integrating AI-driven solutions to optimize their operations and enhance customer interactions.

AI chatbots and virtual assistants have revolutionized how initial contact is made with customers. These advanced systems can handle a high volume of calls simultaneously, providing consistent and accurate information without fatigue or error. For instance, companies like *Conversica* use AI to automate lead follow-up processes, ensuring prompt responses to customer inquiries.

Key AI solutions transforming telemarketing:

- **Natural Language Processing (NLP):** Enables chatbots to understand and respond to customer queries in a human-like manner.

- **Predictive Dialers:** Automatically dial numbers from a

database and connect the call to an available agent once a live person answers.

- **Sentiment Analysis:** Assesses the emotional tone of conversations, allowing for real-time adjustments in communication strategies.

Effectiveness of AI-Driven Sales Calls Compared to Human Agents

The effectiveness of AI-driven sales calls versus human agents sparks much debate among industry professionals. On the one hand, AI systems offer unparalleled efficiency and consistency. They can handle repetitive tasks without the risk of burnout, ensuring that every call adheres to company standards.

However, human agents bring an element of emotional intelligence that AI currently lacks. The ability to read subtle cues in voice tone or adapt conversational techniques based on real-time feedback remains challenging for even the most sophisticated AI systems. Studies by *McKinsey & Company* reveal that while AI can significantly improve productivity in telemarketing, it often works best when complementing rather than replacing human agents.

Comparative insights:

- **Consistency:** AI ensures uniformity in messaging, reducing variance caused by human error.

- **Scalability:** Unlike humans, AI can manage thousands of interactions simultaneously.

- **Empathy:** Human agents excel in building rapport and trust through personalized interactions.

Long-term Outlook for Telemarketers

The long-term outlook for telemarketers hinges on how quickly and effectively organizations adopt these new technologies. While there is an undeniable shift towards automation, this does not spell the end for human telemarketers. Instead, their roles are evolving into more specialized positions that require higher levels of skill and emotional intelligence.

Telemarketers will increasingly focus on complex sales negotiations and relationship-building activities that demand a human touch. Additionally, they will need to work alongside AI tools, leveraging data insights generated by these systems to enhance their performance. As noted by Gartner's research, by 2025, nearly 75% of customer interactions will be managed by both humans and machines working together seamlessly.

Predicted trends:

- **Hybrid Roles:** Combining technical proficiency with strong interpersonal skills.

- **Upskilling Opportunities:** Continuous learning programs to keep pace with technological advancements.

- **Enhanced Customer Experiences:** Using AI data analytics to tailor interactions more effectively.

"AI isn't here to replace us; it's here to augment our capabilities." — Satya Nadella

Research Data:

According to *Forrester Research*, companies implementing AI-driven customer engagement solutions see a 50% increase in lead conversion rates.

High Paying Jobs That AI Can't Touch

Artificial Intelligence (AI) is rapidly transforming the job market. From data processing to customer service, machines are increasingly taking over tasks traditionally performed by humans. This shift brings both opportunities and challenges, particularly the fear of job displacement. Yet, there remain high-paying jobs where human qualities—such as emotional intelligence, creativity, and complex decision-making—are irreplaceable.

Key takeaway: While AI may streamline many processes, there are professions where human attributes remain invaluable. These roles not only offer high compensation but also demand skills that machines cannot replicate.

- The unique human qualities that set us apart from machines.

- High-paying professions resistant to AI replacement.

- Key factors to consider when choosing an AI-resistant career field.

By understanding these elements, you'll be better equipped to navigate the evolving job landscape and secure a future-proof career.

The Rise of AI and Its Implications

Artificial intelligence (AI) has a rich history, with its roots going back to the mid-20th century. Early pioneers like Alan Turing and John McCarthy laid the foundation, imagining machines that could mimic human thinking. Over the years, there have been gradual advancements, but it wasn't until the 21st century that AI truly began to change our world. Rapid progress in machine learning and data analysis has moved AI from theoretical ideas to real-world applications in various fields.

Current Trends in AI and Automation

AI's presence in different industries is clear:

- **Healthcare:** AI-powered diagnostic tools can analyze medical images with remarkable accuracy.

- **Finance:** Algorithms now handle everything from high-frequency trading to fraud detection.

- **Retail:** Personalized shopping experiences are driven by sophisticated recommendation engines.

- **Manufacturing:** Robotics streamline production lines, improving efficiency and reducing costs.

The rise of **job automation** brings both opportunities and challenges. Machines are great at doing repetitive tasks, which leads to higher productivity and cost savings. But this change also raises concerns about people losing their jobs.

The Fear and Fascination Surrounding Job Displacement

The complex story of AI's impact has two sides. On one side, there's excitement about the potential for a highly efficient, automated future. On the other side, there's worry about people becoming irrelevant in their jobs.

Understanding the Duality of AI's Impact

- **Fear:** Many people are worried about mass unemployment and economic inequality. History shows us that when new technologies come along, they often disrupt society—just think of what happened during the Industrial Revolution.

- **Fascination:** The appeal of new ideas keeps society interested. Breakthroughs like natural language processing or self-driving cars create buzz about what lies ahead.

This contrast highlights how crucial it is to pinpoint jobs where human qualities are still essential. As we explore these professions further, it becomes evident why some roles can resist the wave of automation.

Understanding Human Qualities that Set Us Apart from Machines

The human essence is made up of emotional intelligence, creativity, and complex decision-making processes. These qualities distinguish us significantly from the binary logic of machines.

Emotional Intelligence: The Heart of Human Interaction

Emotional intelligence (EI) refers to the ability to recognize, understand, and manage our own emotions while also being able to recognize, understand, and influence the emotions of others. In the workplace, EI is invaluable:

- **Empathy**: Understanding colleagues' feelings fosters a supportive environment.

- **Conflict Resolution**: Navigating interpersonal disputes requires nuanced understanding.

- **Leadership**: Inspiring and motivating teams hinges on emotional connectivity.

Daniel Goleman, a renowned psychologist, highlights that "emotional intelligence can be as important as IQ," particularly in jobs requiring human interaction and leadership.

Creativity: The Spark of Innovation

Creativity ignites innovation and propels industries forward. Machines operate on pre-defined algorithms; humans think outside these boundaries. Creative professionals excel in areas such as:

- **Art and Design**: Originality in visual arts and user experience design.

- **Writing**: Crafting narratives that resonate deeply with audiences.

- **Music**: Composing melodies that evoke profound emotions.

Steve Jobs encapsulated this sentiment when he said, "Creativity is just connecting things." This ability to see connections where none exist for machines fuels groundbreaking advancements.

Decision-Making: The Art of Complex Judgments

Human decision-making involves many factors that algorithms struggle to replicate. Decisions are rarely based on data alone but also intuition, values, and ethical considerations. Key aspects include:

- **Ethical Judgments**: Weighing right versus wrong in complex scenarios.

- **Strategic Thinking**: Long-term planning influenced by unpredictable variables.

- **Adaptability**: Adjusting decisions dynamically based on new information.

These multifaceted processes underscore why roles involving strategic leadership or ethical governance remain firmly within the human domain.

Human qualities bring depth and complexity to our professional lives that AI cannot fully imitate. This unique combination of intellect and emotion ensures certain high-paying jobs remain resistant to automation.

High Paying Jobs Resistant to AI Replacement

1. Medical Professionals: The Empathetic Healers Who Can't Be Replaced

Medical professionals occupy a unique space in the job market, one that is not only high-paying but also resistant to AI encroachment. The healthcare industry thrives on human-centric roles that demand irreplaceable skills and qualities—qualities that are profoundly human.

Overview of the Medical Profession

The medical field encompasses a broad spectrum of professions, ranging from doctors and surgeons to nurses and therapists. What unites these roles is their reliance on emotional intelligence, empathy, and complex decision-making skills. Machines might assist in diagnostics or surgical procedures, but they fall short when it comes to the nuanced care and emotional support that patients require.

Key highlights of the medical profession include:
- **High earning potential:** According to recent data, specialized doctors such as anesthesiologists, surgeons, and cardiologists can earn upwards of $400,000 annually.

- **Job security:** The Bureau of Labor Statistics projects faster-than-average growth for healthcare occupations due to an aging population and increased demand for healthcare services.

- **Human interaction:** Unlike many jobs susceptible to automation, medical professionals engage directly with patients, offering a level of care and understanding that machines cannot replicate.

Examples of Irreplaceable Roles

Doctors: Physicians represent the epitome of expertise combined with compassion. They diagnose illnesses, develop treatment plans, and provide continuous support throughout a patient's recovery journey. For instance:

- **General Practitioners (GPs):** These doctors build long-term relationships with patients, understanding their medical history in depth. This holistic approach is crucial for accurate diagnosis and effective treatment.

- **Surgeons:** While robotic systems like the Da Vinci Surgical System assist in performing surgeries with precision, the final decisions rest with human surgeons who possess the critical thinking required for complex operations.

Nurses: Often considered the backbone of healthcare systems, nurses deliver essential care that extends beyond mere technical tasks. Their role involves:

- **Patient advocacy:** Nurses ensure that patients' needs are met both medically and emotionally. They act as liaisons between doctors and patients' families, providing clarity and comfort during stressful times.

- **Critical care:** In environments like Intensive Care Units (ICUs), nurses make life-saving decisions based on real-time patient data—a task that demands both scientific knowledge and intuitive judgment.

Therapists: Physical therapists, occupational therapists, and mental health counselors work closely with individuals to improve their quality of life. Their roles require:

- **Personalized care plans:** Therapy involves tailored approaches based on each patient's unique circumstances—a process driven by human insight rather than algorithmic predictions.

- **Emotional support:** Mental health professionals offer empathy and understanding as they guide patients through emotional challenges—an area where AI lacks the depth of human experience.

Medical Researchers: Pioneering new treatments and advancing medical science necessitates creative thinking and experimentation—qualities intrinsic to humans. Researchers hypothesize novel ideas, design experiments, interpret complex data sets, and draw nuanced conclusions—tasks beyond current AI capabilities.

Case Study: Dr. Atul Gawande

Dr. Atul Gawande is a renowned surgeon and public health researcher known for his contributions to improving surgical practices worldwide. His work exemplifies how medical professionals blend technical expertise with innovative problem-solving skills:

> "Better is possible. It does not take genius... It takes diligence; it takes moral clarity; it takes ingenuity; and above all it takes a willingness to try." — Dr. Atul Gawande

His emphasis on continuous improvement underscores why medical roles remain resilient against AI replacement: they thrive on proactive adaptation combined with an inherent commitment to patient welfare.

In essence, while AI continues to advance in diagnostic precision or robotic surgery assistance, it falls short in replicating the empathetic healer's role—a complex interplay of compassion, intuition, ethical judgment, and intricate decision-making processes that define medical professionals

2. Legal Professionals: Navigating Complexity with Human Judgment

In the world of *legal professionals*, the complex mix of laws, rules, and human experiences is a place where humans are still more important than machines. The legal profession is a shining example of *job security* because it depends on *unique skills* and *people-focused roles*. Unlike routine tasks that can be automated, the diverse nature of legal work requires a deep understanding of human behavior, societal norms, and ethical considerations.

Lawyers' Ability to Analyze Intricate Cases

Legal professionals have a special skill: they can analyze complicated cases, something AI struggles with. Every legal case has its own complexities and emotions. For instance:

- **Criminal Defense Attorneys** must understand not just the law but also the psychological aspects of representing their clients.

- **Corporate Lawyers** often handle high-stakes negotiations that require them to read between the lines and grasp unspoken intentions.

The ability to provide *nuanced arguments* is another area where lawyers shine. This goes beyond just applying laws; it's about creating persuasive stories that connect with judges and juries. While AI can quickly sift through large amounts of data, it cannot turn these findings into compelling human narratives.

Human Interaction in Legal Proceedings

Courtrooms are places where *humans interact*. Body language, tone of voice, and emotional appeal are all crucial in determining legal outcomes. For example:

> "A lawyer's cross-examination technique can unravel truths or expose lies—tasks that require acute human intuition," says renowned attorney David Boies.

AI may help with research and reviewing documents, but it cannot replace the *empathetic presence* needed during meetings with clients or in court. This human touch is essential for building trust—a key element in lawyer-client relationships.

Decision-Making Under Uncertainty

Legal decisions often happen when things are unclear or uncertain. Lawyers have to look at conflicting pieces of evidence, think about different interpretations, and consider what might happen in the future. This flexible decision-making process involves:

1. Assessing risks

2. Predicting how people will act

3. Creating strategies that can change as situations evolve

These tasks are difficult to automate because they rely on qualities like judgment, experience, and ethical reasoning.

Examples from Notable Figures

Famous figures in law emphasize how important human judgment is in their field. Justice Ruth Bader Ginsburg once said:

> "Judges must decide difficult questions that go be-
> yond black-and-white rules."

Such statements show that while AI can make processes faster, it cannot replace the deep understanding needed for important legal decisions.

Key Takeaway

Legal professionals demonstrate how certain high-paying jobs are still safe from AI disruption because they depend on human intuition, interaction, and judgment. These roles highlight a larger idea: professions that need empathy, creativity, and ethical reasoning will continue to offer strong job security even as automation becomes more common.

By looking at these aspects within the legal profession, we can understand why some careers handle technological advancements better than others.

3. Creative Fields: Where Original Thought Takes Center Stage

Creative professions are a stronghold against the unstoppable rise of automation. While AI can produce art or music, nothing beats the genuine human touch in these fields. The true worth of creativity lies in its unpredictability and emotional depth—qualities that algorithms find hard to replicate.

Writers: Crafting Narratives Beyond Code

Writing is more than just putting words together; it's about creating complex stories filled with thoughts, feelings, and experiences. From novelists to screenwriters, these artists create pieces that resonate deeply with humanity. Take *J.K. Rowling*, for example—her "Harry Potter" series has enchanted millions worldwide with its storytelling brilliance. The subtleties and distinctive viewpoints that writers bring to their work are something machines cannot replace.

Designers: Merging Art and Functionality

In design—be it graphic, fashion, or industrial—human instinct is vital. Think of *Steve Jobs*, who transformed technology with his sharp sense of design and user experience. He understood what people wanted even before they did! This ability to grasp and predict human desires ensures that designers remain essential. Their craft demands both technical expertise and artistic insight, something AI struggles to achieve entirely.

Musicians: Striking a Chord with Human Emotion

Music is more than just sounds; it's a medium for feelings and cultural storytelling. Legendary musicians like *Ludwig van Beethoven* or *Beyoncé* reach out to listeners through their distinct styles and emotional richness. Sure, AI can churn out tunes—but it lacks the essence that comes from lived experiences and genuine emotions. The knack musicians have for spontaneous creativity, groundbreaking ideas, and stirring feelings makes them irreplaceable in this domain.

Why Creative Professions Are Safe from AI

1. **Unpredictability**: Creative fields thrive on originality and unexpected connections that computers find challenging to generate.

2. **Emotional Intelligence**: Understanding human emotions is central to creating impactful art.

3. **Cultural Relevance**: Artists often draw from their cultural backgrounds and personal experiences, adding layers of meaning unattainable by AI.

4. **Human Interaction**: Many creative roles involve collaboration and feedback loops which necessitate nuanced interpersonal skills.

The creative professions highlight the unmatched worth of human intuition, interaction, and innovation—elements that ensure job security in an increasingly automated world.

4. Leadership Roles: Guiding Teams with Strategic Thinking and Interpersonal Skills

Leadership roles are positions that heavily rely on human qualities, making them difficult for AI to replicate. These executive positions require a combination of vision, decision-making skills, and emotional intelligence—qualities that are inherently human and challenging for machines to imitate.

1. Vision and Strategic Thinking

Leaders are visionaries who set the direction for their organizations. They have the ability to see the bigger picture, anticipate market trends, and make strategic decisions that lead to long-term success. This foresight requires a deep understanding of human behavior, market dynamics, and creative thinking—qualities that AI lacks.

> **Example:** Visionary leaders like Steve Jobs transformed industries not only through technical expertise but also through an extraordinary ability to predict future needs and inspire teams to achieve remarkable goals.

2. Decision-Making Skills

The complexity of human decision-making processes is another area where machines struggle. Leaders often encounter ambiguous situations that require nuanced judgment calls beyond simple logic or data analysis.

> **Example:** In crisis management scenarios, a CEO must consider various factors—financial implications, employee morale, public perception—and make quick yet informed decisions. This intricate balancing act highlights the irreplaceable nature of human intuition in leadership roles.

3. Emotional Intelligence

Emotional intelligence (EI) distinguishes exceptional leaders from their peers. It encompasses self-awareness, empathy, social skills, and effective relationship management.

> **Example:** Leaders with high EI create collaborative environments, resolve conflicts amicably, and motivate their teams to excel. While machines can process data efficiently, they lack the ability to genuinely understand and respond to human emotions.

4. Examples of High-Paying Leadership Roles Resistant to AI

Several executive positions exemplify these irreplaceable skills:

- **Chief Executive Officers (CEOs):** Responsible for overall organizational strategy, CEOs must possess unmatched vision and decision-making abilities.

- **Chief Financial Officers (CFOs):** In addition to analyzing numbers, CFOs need strategic insight into financial planning and risk management.

- **Human Resources Directors:** Emotional intelligence is crucial here; HR directors navigate complex interpersonal dynamics and shape company culture.

- **Marketing Executives:** Creativity and deep market understanding enable these leaders to craft compelling narratives that resonate with target audiences.

AI excels at automating tasks but falls short in roles requiring human intuition and interaction. Leadership positions clearly highlight this distinction.

The essential nature of these roles ensures job security in an era increasingly dominated by technology. Identifying high-paying jobs less susceptible to AI replacement involves recognizing the inherent value of uniquely human skills—visionary thinking, nuanced decision-making, and emotional intelligence are at the forefront in leadership roles.

5. Technology Experts: Innovating at the Intersection of Man and Machine

In today's fast-paced world of technology, some jobs in the tech industry offer a sense of security. These roles require both human creativity and technical skills, making them less likely to be taken over by AI.

Data Scientists: The Alchemists of the Digital Age

Data scientists perfectly combine analytical skills with innovative thinking. They analyze large amounts of data to find useful insights, a task that needs not only computer power but also a deep understanding of context and subtlety.

- **Analytical Skills**: While algorithms can process numbers very quickly, it's humans who make sense of these patterns in meaningful ways.

- **Creative Problem Solving**: Data scientists often need to come up with new methods to solve unique problems, something machines find difficult because they lack creative thinking.

Cybersecurity Specialists: Guardians of the Digital Realm

As cyber threats become more complex, cybersecurity specialists are becoming more essential. Their job involves not just technical defenses but also predicting and outsmarting human opponents.

- **Human Intuition**: Spotting potential threats often depends on gut feeling and experience, traits that are inherently human.

- **Adaptability**: Cybersecurity is always changing, needing professionals who can adjust strategies on the fly, something AI struggles with because it relies on pre-set responses.

Software Developers: Architects of Future Innovations

Software development is still an area where human creativity is key. Creating software solutions requires a deep understanding of user needs and imaginative thinking.

- **User-Centric Design**: Developers must understand end-users to create easy-to-use and effective software solutions.

- **Innovation**: The ability to think differently is crucial for developing advanced applications that push technological limits.

"The most important skill in data science is not coding; it's curiosity." — DJ Patil, Former Chief Data Scientist of the U.S. Office of Science and Technology Policy.

"Cybersecurity isn't just about technology; it's about people managing those technologies." — Bruce Schneier, Security Technologist and Author.

Key Takeaways

These technical roles highlight the irreplaceable skills humans bring to the table:

- **Creative Insight**: Whether interpreting data or designing software, human creativity remains a cornerstone.

- **Emotional Intelligence**: Understanding user needs or predicting cybersecurity threats requires empathy and intuition.

- **Adaptability**: Rapidly evolving challenges demand flexible thinking that machines currently cannot replicate.

Exploring these careers reveals a consistent theme—human-centric roles that leverage our unique abilities stand resilient against the tide of automation.

What to Look for in an AI Resistant Career Field

Choosing a profession that stands resilient against the relentless march of AI requires a careful evaluation of certain criteria. These elements help ensure career resilience and adaptability, crucial aspects in an ever-evolving job market.

1. Emphasis on Emotional Intelligence

Professions that demand high levels of emotional intelligence are less likely to be supplanted by machines. Roles that require empathy, understanding, and nuanced human interaction often involve complex emotional dynamics that AI struggles to mimic.

- **Healthcare Professionals**: Doctors and nurses not only diagnose and treat but also provide comfort and emotional support.

- **Counselors and Therapists**: These roles rely heavily on building trust and understanding human emotions.

2. Creativity and Innovation

Fields driven by creativity remain largely insulated from automation. The ability to think outside the box, generate original ideas, and innovate is inherently human.

- **Artists and Designers**: From visual arts to fashion design, these professions thrive on unique creative expressions.

- **Writers and Musicians**: Crafting compelling narratives or composing original music involves a depth of creativity beyond the reach of AI.

3. Complex Decision-Making

Jobs requiring intricate decision-making processes benefit from human judgment and experience. These roles often entail considering various factors, potential outcomes, and ethical implications.

- **Legal Professionals**: Lawyers analyze complex cases, interpret laws, and provide nuanced arguments.

- **Executives and Managers**: Strategic thinking, vision-setting, and leadership are central to these positions.

4. Interpersonal Skills

Roles that depend on building relationships and influencing people are harder for AI to replicate effectively. Human connections play a pivotal role in such careers.

- **Sales Executives**: Success in sales often hinges on building rapport with clients.

- **Public Relations Specialists**: Managing public perception requires adept interpersonal skills.

5. Technical Expertise with a Human Touch

While technology-related fields evolve rapidly, those at the intersection of human creativity and technical expertise maintain a significant edge.

- **Cybersecurity Specialists**: Protecting systems from complex threats necessitates both technical skills and adaptive thinking.

- **Data Scientists**: Interpreting vast amounts of data requires not just algorithmic knowledge but also insight into human behavior patterns.

To navigate the shifting sands of the job market effectively, focus on careers where uniquely human qualities—emotional intelligence, creativity, complex decision-making, interpersonal skills—are indispensable. Identifying these traits within your chosen field can provide a robust defense against the encroachment of AI technologies.

Jobs and Careers That AI Can't Easily Replace

- **Surgeon** - Requires complex decision-making and manual dexterity that AI can't replicate.

- **Psychiatrist** - Involves deep human interaction and understanding of mental health.

- **Anesthesiologist** - Needs precise real-time adjustments and patient monitoring.

- **Dentist** - Combines technical skill and patient care that AI cannot fully automate.

- **Orthodontist** - Requires personalized treatment plans and manual adjustments.

- **Optometrist** - Involves patient interaction and personalized eye care.

- **Pharmacist** - Requires professional judgment and patient counseling.

- **Veterinarian** - Involves hands-on care and diagnosis of animals.

- **Physician Assistant** - Requires patient interaction and clinical decision-making.

- **Nurse Practitioner** - Involves personalized patient care and health management.

- **Physical Therapist** - Requires tailored treatment plans and hands-on therapy.

- **Occupational Therapist** - Involves customized care plans and patient interaction.

- **Speech-Language Pathologist** - Requires personalized therapy and human interaction.

- **Radiation Therapist** - Involves patient-specific treatment and monitoring.

- **Chiropractor** - Requires manual adjustments and personalized care.

- **Clinical Laboratory Technician** - Involves complex analysis and interpretation of lab results.

- **Biomedical Engineer** - Requires innovative problem-solving and design skills.

- **Environmental Engineer** - Involves complex problem-solving and regulatory compliance.

- **Civil Engineer** - Requires creative design and project management.

- **Aerospace Engineer** - Involves innovative design and testing of aerospace systems.

- **Electrical Engineer** - Requires complex problem-solving and design skills.

- **Mechanical Engineer** - Involves creative design and engineering solutions.

- **Chemical Engineer** - Requires innovative process design and safety management.

- **Software Developer** - Involves creative problem-solving and design of software solutions.

- **Data Scientist** - Requires advanced analytical skills and interpretation of data.

- **Cybersecurity Analyst** - Involves dynamic problem-solving and threat management.

- **Information Systems Manager** - Requires strategic planning and management of IT systems.

- **IT Project Manager** - Involves managing complex projects and human resources.

- **Network Architect** - Requires advanced design and optimization of networks.

- **Database Administrator** - Involves complex database management and security.

- **Market Research Analyst** - Requires human insight into market trends and consumer behavior.

- **Financial Analyst** - Involves complex financial analysis and strategic recommendations.

- **Actuary** - Requires advanced mathematical skills and risk assessment.

- **Personal Financial Advisor** - Involves personalized financial planning and advice.

- **Management Consultant** - Requires human insight into organizational improvement.

- **HR Manager** - Involves managing human resources and complex interpersonal issues.

- **Sales Manager** - Requires human interaction and strategic sales planning.

- **Marketing Manager** - Involves creative strategy and market understanding.

- **Operations Manager** - Requires dynamic problem-solving and process optimization.

- **Construction Manager** - Involves project management and on-site decision-making.

- **Project Manager** - Requires coordination of complex projects and human resources.

- **Real Estate Manager** - Involves personalized client interactions and property management.

- **Public Relations Specialist** - Requires strategic communication and human interaction.

- **Lawyer** - Involves complex legal analysis and client advocacy.

- **Judge** - Requires human judgment and interpretation of the law.

- **Legislator** - Involves human insight and decision-making in policymaking.

- **School Principal** - Requires management of educational staff and student interactions.

- **University Professor** - Involves personalized teaching and academic research.

- **Special Education Teacher** - Requires individualized teaching and student care.

- **Therapist/Counselor** - Involves deep human interaction and personalized therapy.

- **Respiratory Therapist** - Requires patient-specific care and manual respiratory treatments.

- **Dietitian/Nutritionist** - Involves personalized dietary planning and counseling.

- **Art Director** - Requires creative vision and artistic skills.

- **Graphic Designer** - Involves creative design and visual communication.

- **Interior Designer** - Requires personalized design solutions and client interaction.

- **Urban Planner** - Involves complex planning and human-centered design.

- **Archaeologist** - Requires human interpretation of artifacts and historical sites.

- **Historian** - Involves research and interpretation of historical events and documents.

- **Psychologist** - Requires deep understanding of human behavior and mental health.

- **Audiologist** - Involves personalized hearing assessments and treatments.

- **Genetic Counselor** - Requires interpreting genetic information and counseling patients.

- **Sociologist** - Involves studying social behavior and human interactions.

- **Anthropologist** - Requires human-centered research and cultural analysis.

- **Museum Curator** - Involves preserving and interpreting artifacts and artworks.

- **Librarian** - Requires managing information and assisting patrons.

- **Event Planner** - Involves coordinating and personalizing events and gatherings.

- **Chef/Head Cook** - Requires culinary creativity and hands-on food preparation.

- **Sommelier** - Involves expert knowledge of wines and personalized recommendations.

- **Barber/Hairdresser** - Requires personalized hair care and styling.

- **Esthetician** - Involves personalized skincare treatments and client interaction.

- **Jeweler** - Requires manual craftsmanship and creative design.

- **Florist** - Involves creative floral design and personalized arrangements.

- **Fashion Designer** - Requires creative vision and manual garment creation.

- **Furniture Maker** - Involves skilled craftsmanship and personalized designs.

- **Landscape Architect** - Requires creative design and environmental planning.

- **Marine Biologist** - Involves field research and complex data analysis.

- **Forestry Manager** - Requires managing natural resources and environmental planning.

- **Zoologist** - Involves studying animal behavior and ecosystems.

- **Wildlife Biologist** - Requires field research and species conservation efforts.

- **Park Ranger** - Involves managing natural parks and human interaction.

- **Agricultural Scientist** - Requires research and innovation in farming practices.

- **Horticulturist** - Involves plant cultivation and personalized landscaping.

- **Meteorologist** - Requires weather prediction and complex data interpretation.

- **Astronomer** - Involves studying celestial objects and interpreting data.

- **Geologist** - Requires field research and interpretation of geological data.

- **Marine Engineer** - Involves designing and maintaining marine equipment and vessels.

- **Ship Captain** - Requires navigation and management of maritime operations.

- **Air Traffic Controller** - Involves real-time decision-making and managing flight operations.

- **Pilot** - Requires manual flying skills and real-time decision-making.

- **Paramedic** - Involves emergency medical care and patient interaction.

- **Firefighter** - Requires physical skills and real-time decision-making.

- **Police Officer** - Involves law enforcement and complex human interactions.

- **Detective/Criminal Investigator** - Requires solving crimes and human intuition.

- **Correctional Officer** - Involves managing inmate populations and maintaining order.

- **Security Specialist** - Requires real-time threat assessment and management.

- **Emergency Management Director** - Involves planning and responding to emergencies.

- **Speechwriter** - Requires personalized writing and creative communication skills.

- **Public Health Administrator** - Involves managing health programs and community interaction.

- **Nonprofit Manager** - Requires managing nonprofit organizations and human resources.

- **Clergy/Pastor** - Involves spiritual guidance and deep human interaction.

Transitioning to AI-Resistant Jobs

What Are Transferable Skills?

Transferable skills are the abilities and knowledge that can be applied across different jobs and industries. These skills are not specific to a particular role, providing flexibility in a constantly changing job market. Unlike technical skills, which may become outdated as technology evolves, transferable skills remain valuable over time. They serve as a foundation upon which professionals can build new competencies, making them essential for anyone looking to transition into jobs that are less likely to be affected by AI.

Why Are Transferable Skills Important in Today's Job Market?

The modern workforce requires adaptability and resilience. As artificial intelligence continues to reshape industries, jobs that were once secure are now at risk of being automated. The World Economic Forum predicts that by 2025, machines will perform more tasks than humans in some sectors. This shift highlights the significance of transferable skills, enabling individuals to smoothly transition from roles vulnerable to automation to those that require uniquely human abilities.

Key Traits of Transferable Skills

- **Adaptability**: The ability to quickly adjust to new technologies and methods.

- **Resilience**: The mental strength needed to navigate career changes and industry disruptions.

Examples of Transferable Skills That Are Useful for Jobs Less Likely to Be Affected by AI

Several transferable skills stand out as particularly relevant for roles less likely to be affected by AI:

1. **Critical Thinking**: The ability to analyze complex problems, evaluate evidence, and make informed decisions is irreplaceable by AI. This skill is essential for roles in management, strategy, and research.

2. **Emotional Intelligence (EQ)**: Understanding and managing one's emotions, as well as empathizing with others, plays a significant role in leadership and customer-facing positions. High EQ fosters better teamwork and conflict resolution.

3. **Communication**: Effective verbal and written communication is vital for collaboration across various functions within an organization. It ensures that ideas are clearly conveyed and understood.

4. **Problem-Solving**: The ability to devise innovative solutions when faced with unexpected challenges is a hallmark of human ingenuity that AI struggles to replicate.

5. **Leadership**: Guiding teams through change, motivating individuals, and managing projects require a human touch that technology cannot emulate.

6. **Creativity**: Generating original ideas and thinking outside the box are quintessential human traits that drive innovation in fields such as marketing, design, and R&D.

7. **Time Management**: Prioritizing tasks effectively ensures productivity remains high even when workloads are substantial.

These examples show how transferable skills support roles resistant to automation by leveraging traits uniquely human in nature.

Real-Life Examples of Transferable Skills in Action

Consider the case of Satya Nadella, CEO of Microsoft. His rise within Microsoft can be attributed not only to his technical expertise but also his strong leadership qualities and emotional intelligence—both transferable skills crucial in guiding a tech giant through waves of innovation.

In another scenario, Sarah Blakely founded Spanx by combining creativity with effective problem-solving strategies when designing her first prototype using a pair of scissors on pantyhose. Her success story underscores how creativity remains unchallenged by AI advancements.

How Can You Develop Your Transferable Skills?

Investing time in improving these skills can significantly boost career prospects in an AI-dominated future. Here are some ways you can develop your transferable skills:

- Attend workshops or seminars focused on specific skills you want to improve.

- Enroll in online courses or certification programs related to your field.

- Seek mentorship from experienced professionals who can guide you in developing these attributes.

- Join networking groups or communities where you can learn from others' experiences.

By incorporating these qualities into their professional toolkit, individuals can navigate the complexities of evolving industries with greater ease while remaining valuable assets within their organizations.

Building a Personalized Learning Plan

Creating a personalized learning plan is like navigating through unknown waters. Tailoring your educational journey requires a mix of self-reflection, strategy, and resourcefulness. Personalized learning not only enhances skill acquisition but also aligns your growth trajectory with evolving job market demands.

Steps to Create a Learning Plan

1. **Self-Assessment**: Begin with a thorough self-assessment. Identify your strengths, weaknesses, interests, and career aspirations. Tools like SWOT analysis (Strengths, Weaknesses, Opportunities, Threats) can provide valuable insights.

2. **Set Clear Goals**: Define specific, measurable, achievable, relevant, and time-bound (SMART) goals. For instance, if you aim to transition into data science, set clear milestones for mastering Python or completing relevant certifications.

3. **Research Market Trends**: Investigate current job market trends to understand which skills are in demand. Use platforms like LinkedIn and Glassdoor to analyze job postings and identify common requirements.

4. **Skill Gap Analysis**: Compare your current skill set with the skills required for your desired role. This will highlight any gaps that need addressing.

5. **Develop a Timeline**: Create a realistic timeline for achieving each goal. Break down larger objectives into smaller tasks to maintain motivation and track progress effectively.

Aligning Personal Goals with Job Market Demands

Personal aspirations must be harmonized with market realities to ensure relevance and employability:

- **Industry Research**: Stay informed about industry developments by subscribing to newsletters, following thought leaders on social media, and joining relevant forums.

- **Networking**: Engage with professionals in your target field through networking events or online communities. Their insights can offer invaluable guidance on aligning personal goals with market needs.

- **Flexibility**: Remain adaptable as industry demands evolve. Continuous reevaluation of goals ensures alignment with emerging trends.

Utilizing Resources Effectively

The modern learner has access to an unprecedented array of resources:

- **Online Courses**: Platforms like Coursera, Udemy, and Khan Academy offer courses across various disciplines. These are often designed by industry experts and provide flexibility for learners.

- **Books and Journals**: Traditional resources remain invaluable. Books by industry leaders or academic journals provide deep dives into specific subjects.

- **Mentorship Programs**: Seeking mentorship from experienced professionals can accelerate learning by providing personalized advice and industry insights.

- **Workshops and Seminars**: Attending workshops allows for hands-on experience and direct interaction with experts in the field.

- **Practice Projects**: Apply new knowledge through practical projects or internships to gain real-world experience.

As you craft your personalized learning plan, think of it as building a bridge between where you are now and where you aspire to be professionally. Each step taken is a plank laid down towards your future success in AI-resistant careers.

Importance of Critical Thinking and Problem Solving

Why Critical Thinking Matters in Jobs That AI Can't Replace

In today's digital world, machines and algorithms can handle repetitive tasks very well. But when it comes to making complex decisions, planning strategies, and adapting to new situations, humans still have a big advantage. This is where critical thinking becomes crucial.

Critical thinking is the ability to look at information objectively and make logical decisions. In jobs that AI can't replace, this skill is essential for a few reasons:

- **Making Complex Decisions**: While AI can provide data and predictions, understanding these insights requires human interpretation. Whether it's predicting financial trends or diagnosing medical conditions, professionals need to consider various factors and possible outcomes.

- **Planning Strategically**: Long-term business plans often rely on unpredictable elements like market feelings or changes in regulations. Critical thinkers are good at imagining different future scenarios and creating strong plans.

- **Considering Ethics**: Decisions involving moral dilemmas shouldn't be left solely to algorithms. For example, in fields like healthcare or law enforcement, it's important to understand the ethical implications of actions.

Ways to Improve Your Problem-Solving Skills

Improving your problem-solving abilities means using specific methods and habits that promote analytical thinking:

1. **Root Cause Analysis (RCA)**:

- This technique helps you find the main cause of a problem instead of just treating its symptoms.

1. **SWOT Analysis (Strengths, Weaknesses, Opportunities, Threats)**:

- Useful for strategic planning by looking at internal and external factors affecting an organization or project.

1. **Brainstorming Sessions**:

- Encourages creative thinking by letting team members suggest different solutions without immediate criticism.

1. **Mind Mapping**:

- Visual representation of problems and potential solutions helps in organizing thoughts and recognizing patterns.

1. **Scenario Planning**:

- Developing different future scenarios aids in preparing for uncertainties.

Examples from Industry Leaders Who Use Critical Thinking

Industry leaders show us how critical thinking and problem-solving skills lead to meaningful results:

- **Elon Musk**, CEO of SpaceX and Tesla, is known for his innovative approach to solving difficult problems like space travel and sustainable energy. He breaks down huge challenges into smaller parts—known as first principles thinking—to come up with new ideas.

- **Indra Nooyi**, former CEO of PepsiCo, showed remarkable critical thinking during her time as leader. By predicting market shifts towards healthier lifestyles, she led PepsiCo's transformation towards healthier products long before it became popular among other companies.

- **Satya Nadella**, CEO of Microsoft, revived the company by promoting a culture of continuous learning and reevaluating past strategies. His emphasis on cloud computing was a direct result of studying industry changes and spotting new opportunities early on.

These examples prove that critical thinking isn't just something you learn in school; it's a practical skill that brings about significant change within organizations.

Critical thinking and analytical skills are essential qualities that distinguish human abilities from automated systems. As industries evolve alongside technological progress, these inherent human traits will become even more valuable.

Developing Emotional Intelligence and Empathy

Significance of Emotional Intelligence in the Workplace

Emotional intelligence (EI) is a valuable skill in today's workplace. It involves being able to recognize, understand, and manage our own emotions, as well as effectively handling relationships with others. According to Daniel Goleman, a well-known psychologist, EI is often more important than IQ in determining success both personally and professionally. While AI is powerful, it lacks the nuanced understanding of human emotions, making EI an essential skill in jobs that are less likely to be automated.

Methods to Cultivate Empathy

Cultivating empathy requires deliberate practice and mindfulness. Here are some effective methods:

- **Active Listening**: Engage fully with colleagues by paying attention to their words, tone, and body language. Reflecting back what you hear can validate their feelings.

- **Perspective-Taking**: Try to see situations from others' viewpoints. This can help in understanding their motivations and emotions.

- **Mindfulness Practices**: Techniques such as meditation or journaling can enhance self-awareness and emotional regulation.

- **Feedback Mechanisms**: Encourage open communication where team members can share their feelings and experiences without fear of judgment.

Impact on Team Dynamics and Leadership

Emotional intelligence significantly enhances team dynamics. Leaders with high EI typically foster environments of trust and cooperation. They are adept at resolving conflicts amicably and inspiring their teams through empathy-driven leadership.

Consider Satya Nadella, CEO of Microsoft, who transformed the company culture through an emphasis on empathy. Under his leadership, Microsoft shifted from a "know-it-all" to a "learn-it-all" mindset, promoting continuous learning and mutual respect.

Empathy within teams leads to:

- **Improved Collaboration**: Empathetic team members communicate better and work more cohesively.

- **Higher Job Satisfaction**: When employees feel understood and valued, job satisfaction levels rise.

- **Enhanced Innovation**: A supportive environment encourages creativity and out-of-the-box thinking.

In roles that are less likely to be affected by AI, these interpersonal skills set humans apart from machines. While AI can process data quickly, it cannot replicate the deep emotional connections that drive successful teamwork and leadership.

> "Leadership is not about being in charge. It's about taking care of those in your charge." - Simon Sinek

The development of emotional intelligence and empathy is crucial for thriving in jobs that are less likely to be automated. These skills not only enhance individual performance but also contribute positively to team dynamics and leadership qualities.

Acquiring Advanced Technical Skills

Mastering advanced technical skills is crucial for success in roles that are less likely to be affected by AI. As automation and AI continue to change industries, there will always be a strong demand for specialized skills that machines find difficult to replicate or perform efficiently. In this section, we will explore the specific skills that are currently in demand, the resources available for acquiring these skills, and real-life examples of individuals who have successfully transitioned their careers.

In-Demand Technical Skills for AI-Resistant Roles

1. Data Science and Machine Learning

Understanding data science and machine learning is crucial. While AI can process vast amounts of data, human oversight ensures the ethical and strategic use of insights derived from this data. Key competencies include:

- **Statistical Analysis**

- **Programming Languages (Python, R)**

- **Machine Learning Algorithms**

2. Cybersecurity

With the increasing complexity of cyber threats, cybersecurity experts play a critical role in safeguarding digital assets. Skills in high demand encompass:

- **Threat Intelligence**

- **Network Security**

- **Incident Response**

3. Software Development

While some aspects of software development can be automated, creative problem-solving and complex project management still require a human touch. Essential skills include:

- **Object-Oriented Programming (Java, C++)**

- **Full Stack Development**

- **Agile Methodologies**

Resources for Acquiring Technical Knowledge

Pursuing these skills necessitates access to quality educational resources. The digital age offers various platforms for continuous learning:

- **Online Courses and Tutorials:** Platforms like Coursera, Udemy, and edX provide courses taught by industry experts.

- **Bootcamps:** Intensive coding bootcamps such as General Assembly or Flatiron School offer immersive experiences.

- **Open Source Projects:** Contributing to projects on GitHub can provide practical experience.

For those looking to dive into cybersecurity, resources such as Cybrary and SANS Institute offer comprehensive training programs.

Case Studies of Successful Transitions

1. Jane Doe: From Marketing to Data Science

Jane Doe transitioned from a marketing analyst role to a data scientist within three years. She leveraged online courses from Coursera to gain foundational knowledge in Python and machine learning. Jane then applied her learning by developing predictive models for her company's marketing strategies, showcasing her ability to translate theoretical knowledge into practical applications.

2. John Smith: From IT Support to Cybersecurity Analyst

John Smith's journey from IT support technician to cybersecurity analyst underscores the importance of hands-on experience. He started by obtaining certifications like CompTIA Security+ and CISSP. Volunteering at local non-profits provided John with real-world scenarios to apply his skills, eventually leading to a full-time position as a cybersecurity analyst at a major firm.

These narratives highlight the transformative power of targeted skill acquisition coupled with practical application. The pathway to mastering advanced technical skills involves a combination of structured learning and experiential opportunities.

Understanding which technical skills are valued in AI-resistant roles enables professionals to navigate their career paths strategically. By tapping into diverse educational resources and drawing inspiration from successful transitions, individuals can equip themselves with the expertise required to thrive amidst evolving technological landscapes.

Pursuing Relevant Degrees and Certifications

Overview of Relevant Educational Pathways

In the quest for AI-resistant jobs, pursuing relevant degrees provides a solid foundation upon which technical and non-technical skills can be built. Degrees in fields such as **Human Resources**, **Psychology**, **Ed-**

ucation, and **Healthcare** are less susceptible to automation due to their inherently human-centric nature.

1. Human Resources (HR)

This field focuses on managing employee relations, recruitment, and organizational development. HR professionals require strong inter-personal skills and an understanding of complex human behaviors.

2. Psychology

A background in psychology is invaluable for roles involving mental health, counseling, and human behavior analysis. These areas demand empathy, critical thinking, and a deep understanding of the human psyche.

3. Education

Teaching and educational administration involve nurturing and de-veloping human potential. This field benefits from degrees in Educa-tion or specialized subject areas combined with pedagogical training.

4. Healthcare

Degrees in Nursing, Medicine, or Occupational Therapy prepare individuals for roles that require direct patient interaction, deci-sion-making under uncertainty, and compassionate care.

Value of Certifications in Technology Fields

Certifications serve as verifiable proof of expertise and practical knowledge in specific areas. They are particularly valuable in technology fields where continuous advancements necessitate up-to-date skills. Unlike traditional degrees that may cover broad theoretical concepts, certifications focus on specialized competencies crucial for immediate application in the workplace.

1. **Relevance**: Certifications ensure that professionals remain current with industry standards and technological advancements.

2. **Credibility**: They provide a benchmark of quality and reliability that employers trust.

3. **Flexibility**: Many certifications offer flexible learning schedules, making it easier for professionals to balance work and study.

Examples of Respected Certifications

Gaining certifications from reputed organizations enhances one's career prospects significantly. Below are examples of respected certifications across various domains:

- **Project Management Professional (PMP)**: Offered by the Project Management Institute (PMI), this certification is ideal for those looking to excel in project management roles across diverse industries.

- *"The PMP certification demonstrates that you have the experience, education, and competency to lead and direct projects."* — PMI

- **Certified Information Systems Security Professional (CISSP)**: Provided by (ISC)², this certification is highly regarded in cybersecurity circles. It validates expertise in information security practices and principles.

- *"CISSP is the gold standard for security certifications."* — Forbes

- **Google Analytics Individual Qualification (GAIQ)**: This certification showcases proficiency in using Google Analytics to analyze data effectively—a skill crucial for digital marketing roles.

- *"Data is the new oil."* — Clive Humby

- **AWS Certified Solutions Architect – Associate**: Amazon Web Services (AWS) offers this certification to validate cloud architecture expertise—a critical skill as businesses migrate to cloud platforms.

Across these examples lies a common thread: they signify dedication to professional development and mastery over complex subjects. By strategically choosing degrees and certifications aligned with market demands, one not only stays relevant but also gains a competitive edge in an AI-driven world.

Next steps involve exploring how hands-on experience through internships and volunteering can further cement these academic credentials into real-world practice.

Gaining Experience through Internships and Volunteering

Importance of Hands-On Experience in Career Transition

In today's fast-changing job market, practical experience often matters more than theoretical knowledge. Internships and volunteering offer a valuable way to gain hands-on experience, bridging the gap between what you learn in school and how it applies in the real world. This kind of learning not only improves your skills but also makes you more appealing to employers who value **proven abilities** over just academic qualifications.

A study by the National Association of Colleges and Employers (NACE) found that students with internship experience were more likely to secure full-time employment within six months of graduation compared to their peers without such experience. This underscores the critical role that practical exposure plays in successful career transitions.

How to Find Opportunities in Your Field of Interest

Securing internships or volunteer positions can be daunting, but a strategic approach simplifies the process:

1. **Research:** Identify organizations in your field of interest. Use professional networks like LinkedIn to find companies actively seeking interns or volunteers.

2. **Tailor Applications:** Customize your resume and cover letter for each application to highlight relevant skills and experiences.

3. **Leverage Educational Institutions:** Universities often have dedicated career services that connect students with internship opportunities.

4. **Online Platforms:** Websites like Internships.com, Handshake, and Indeed offer numerous listings tailored to various industries.

5. **Networking Events:** Attend industry conferences and workshops to meet professionals who can provide leads on potential opportunities.

Example: Jane, a recent computer science graduate, utilized her university's career services to land an internship at a leading tech company. Her hands-on experience with software development during this internship significantly boosted her employability.

Networking Benefits through Volunteering

Volunteering offers more than just altruistic satisfaction; it is a powerful networking tool that can lead to unexpected career opportunities. Engaging in volunteer work allows you to connect with like-minded professionals and industry leaders who share your passion.

Building Relationships

Volunteering helps you build meaningful relationships within your industry, which can be beneficial when seeking job recommendations or mentorship.

Showcasing Skills

It provides a platform to demonstrate your skills and work ethic in a less formal setting, making it easier for professionals to notice your capabilities.

Exploring Interests

Volunteering can also help you explore different roles within your field, giving you a clearer understanding of where your strengths lie.

Quote: As Steve Jobs once said, "The only way to do great work is to love what you do." Volunteering allows you to pursue what you love while simultaneously positioning yourself for future career success.

For instance, John, an aspiring marketer, volunteered for several non-profit organizations focused on digital campaigns. His volunteer work caught the attention of a marketing director at one of these organizations, leading to an offer for a paid position.

In essence, both internships and volunteering serve as critical stepping stones towards achieving long-term career goals. They provide practical experience that complements academic knowledge while offering unparalleled networking opportunities that can propel your career forward.

Networking and Professional Associations

Strategies for Effective Networking in the Digital Age

Building a strong network is essential for professional growth. In today's interconnected world, effective networking goes beyond borders, using digital platforms to create meaningful connections. Here are some strategies to boost your networking efforts:

1. Leverage Social Media

Platforms like LinkedIn offer unparalleled opportunities to connect with industry leaders. Engage with posts, share insightful content, and join relevant groups to enhance your visibility.

2. Attend Virtual Meetups and Webinars

Participate in online meetups and webinars that focus on your area of interest. These events often provide breakout sessions for more intimate networking opportunities.

3. Build Your Personal Brand

Cultivate a strong personal brand by consistently sharing knowledge and showcasing expertise through blogs, videos, or podcasts. This positions you as a thought leader in your field.

4. Reach Out Directly

Don't shy away from reaching out directly to professionals you admire. A well-crafted message expressing genuine interest can open doors to valuable conversations.

Benefits of Joining Professional Associations

Professional associations play a crucial role in career growth, offering numerous benefits that go beyond just paying membership fees. Here's why joining these organizations is a smart move:

1. Access Exclusive Resources

Members often enjoy exclusive access to industry reports, research papers, and educational resources that can enhance their professional knowledge.

2. Attend Networking Events

Regular events, conferences, and seminars organized by these associations provide fertile ground for building connections with like-minded professionals.

3. Participate in Career Development Programs

Many associations offer mentorship programs, certification courses, and training sessions designed to accelerate career progression.

4. Boost Your Credibility

Being part of a reputable association adds an extra layer of credibility to your professional profile, often making you more attractive to employers.

Success Stories from Industry Connections

The transformative power of networking is best illustrated through real-life success stories. Consider Jane Doe's journey:

"I joined the Association of Marketing Professionals (AMP) two years ago. Through AMP's mentorship program, I connected with Susan Smith, a veteran in the field. Her guidance helped me navigate complex projects at work. Eventually, Susan introduced me to John Brown at an industry conference, leading directly to my current role as a Senior Marketing Manager."

John Brown's experience highlights another aspect:

"As an active member of the Software Developers Guild (SDG), I attended numerous workshops and panel discussions. It was during one such event that I met Lisa Turner. Our shared interests led us to collaborate on an innovative project that caught the eye of potential investors. Today, we co-own a successful tech startup."

These stories emphasize how strategic networking and being part of professional associations can help achieve career goals.

The connection between networking/associations and ongoing professional development efforts is important to understand here too! Each connection made through networking or associations not only enhances personal growth but also reinforces the critical skills discussed previously—such as emotional intelligence and advanced technical abilities—ensuring one's resilience in an AI-dominated landscape.

This relationship between personal engagement (networking/associations) and continuous learning creates a feedback loop that is vital for sustained career success!

Staying Updated with Industry Trends and Continuous Learning

Industry trends are crucial in the ever-changing world of technology and business. Understanding their significance is like steering a ship through stormy seas—ignoring them can leave you lost, while being aware ensures a steady path towards career advancement.

Why It's Important to Know About Technological Changes

Technological changes influence the job market, redefine roles, and create new opportunities. Being aware of these shifts keeps you competitive. For example, the rapid growth of artificial intelligence has led to new positions like AI ethics specialists and machine learning engineers, roles that didn't exist ten years ago.

Understanding **industry trends** offers several benefits:

- **Anticipating Changes**: Predict shifts in demand for specific skills.

- **Identifying Opportunities**: Spot emerging fields and niches.

- **Staying Competitive**: Maintain relevance by updating your skillset.

This reminds us of how *Blockbuster* failed to see the digital streaming trend led by *Netflix*. This mistake highlights the need for constant awareness.

Resources for Keeping Up with Industry Changes

Staying updated on industry trends requires using various resources. Here are some effective tools:

Blogs

Blogs provide timely insights from industry experts and enthusiasts. Some reliable sources include:

- **TechCrunch**: Focuses on startups and technology news.

- **Harvard Business Review's Technology Section**: Provides in-depth analyses of technological impacts on business.

Reading blogs is like having a casual chat with thought leaders over coffee, getting direct access to their views.

Podcasts

Podcasts offer another engaging way to stay informed. Listening during commutes or workouts can turn free time into productive learning moments. Notable podcasts include:

- **The Vergecast**: Covers consumer tech and industry developments.

- **a16z Podcast**: From venture capital firm Andreessen Horowitz, offers deep dives into tech trends.

Think of podcasts as modern-day conversations by the fireplace where experts share stories and insights in an interesting format.

News Aggregators

News aggregators like *Feedly* collect articles from various sources, allowing personalized news feeds based on interests. Setting up alerts for keywords like "AI-resistant jobs" or "technological advancements" ensures relevant updates reach you promptly.

Online Communities

Platforms like *Reddit* (e.g., r/technology) and professional networks such as *LinkedIn* groups facilitate discussions around current trends. Engaging in these communities can provide diverse viewpoints and foster deeper understanding.

The Need for Continuous Learning

Continuous learning is essential in today's fast-paced world. It involves adopting a mindset where acquiring knowledge is an ongoing process rather than a fixed target.

Strategies for Continuous Learning

1. **Enroll in Online Courses**: Websites like Coursera, edX, and Udacity offer courses ranging from basic coding to advanced AI applications.

2. **Attend Webinars**: Webinars hosted by industry leaders provide real-time learning opportunities without geographical constraints.

3. **Read Books and Journals**: Explore books like "The Innovator's Dilemma" by Clayton Christensen or journals such as MIT Technology Review for comprehensive insights.

4. **Participate in Workshops**: Hands-on workshops enhance practical skills through interactive sessions.

5. **Join Study Groups**: Collaborating with peers encourages knowledge sharing and collective problem-solving.

Real-Life Example: Elon Musk

Elon Musk embodies the spirit of continuous learning. Despite his success with companies like Tesla and SpaceX, Musk spends time reading extensively across various fields—from physics to computer science—constantly broadening his knowledge base to innovate further.

Embracing continuous learning means being flexible and forward-thinking, qualities that are essential in navigating the complexities of modern careers.

Staying updated with industry trends along with a commitment to continuous learning equips professionals with the tools necessary for thriving amidst constant change.

Emphasizing Creativity and Innovation Strategies in AI-Resistant Jobs

Creativity is a strong defense against the rise of artificial intelligence in many job sectors. Machines are great at repetitive tasks, analyzing data, and even solving complex problems, but they still can't match the human ability for original thought and creativity. This unique human trait allows people to innovate, adapt, and come up with solutions that machines can't think of.

The Role of Creativity in AI-Resistant Jobs

Jobs that resist automation often require a high degree of creative thinking. Consider roles in marketing, product design, and strategic planning. These positions demand the ability to think outside the box, generate new ideas, and devise novel approaches to challenges.

1. Marketing Professionals

They craft compelling narratives and campaigns that resonate on an emotional level with audiences—something algorithms struggle to achieve.

2. Product Designers

They blend aesthetics with functionality, creating products that are not just useful but also emotionally engaging.

3. Strategic Planners

They anticipate market trends and develop long-term plans that require foresight and inventive thinking.

The necessity for creativity extends beyond traditionally 'creative' roles. Engineers, scientists, and even financial analysts can benefit from a creative mindset. For instance, engineers might find innovative ways to solve technical problems or optimize processes. Financial analysts could develop unique investment strategies based on emerging market trends.

Techniques to Foster Innovative Thinking

Innovation is not merely an innate talent; it can be cultivated through deliberate practice and strategic techniques:

1. **Mind Mapping**: This technique involves visually organizing information around a central concept. It encourages free-flowing ideas and helps identify connections between disparate thoughts.

2. **Brainstorming Sessions**: Collaborative brainstorming can lead to a multitude of ideas. Setting aside judgment during the idea-generation phase ensures a free flow of creativity.

3. **SCAMPER Technique**: SCAMPER stands for Substitute, Combine, Adapt, Modify, Put to another use, Eliminate, and Reverse. This method prompts individuals to think about problems from different angles.

4. **Cross-Pollination**: Exposing oneself to diverse fields can spark innovative ideas. For example, a software engineer might draw inspiration from biology or art.

5. **Design Thinking Workshops**: These structured sessions guide participants through stages of empathy, definition, ideation, prototyping, and testing.

Real-Life Examples of Creative Innovation

Several industry leaders exemplify how creativity drives innovation:

- **Steve Jobs (Apple)**: His emphasis on design aesthetics and user experience revolutionized consumer electronics.

- **Elon Musk (Tesla/SpaceX)**: His ventures combine technical prowess with imaginative vision—electric vehicles and space travel redefined.

- **Indra Nooyi (PepsiCo)**: Her leadership saw the introduction of healthier product lines in response to changing consumer preferences.

These examples illustrate that fostering creativity isn't just beneficial; it's imperative for staying competitive in an AI-dominated landscape.

Integrating Creativity into Daily Workflow

Embedding creative practices into daily routines can yield substantial benefits:

- **Daily Journaling**: Recording thoughts and ideas each day helps clear the mind and capture fleeting inspirations.

- **Scheduled Reflection Time**: Allocating time for reflection allows for deeper thinking about ongoing projects or potential innovations.

- **Diverse Collaboration Teams**: Working with people from varied backgrounds fosters a melting pot of ideas.

- **Continuous Learning**: Engaging with new courses or workshops keeps the mind fresh and open to novel concepts.

Creativity is more than just an abstract skill; it is a concrete asset that enhances employability in an era increasingly dominated by artificial intelligence. By actively nurturing innovative thinking strategies within one's professional life, individuals can secure their place in AI-resistant roles while driving progress within their industries.

Attending Workshops and Conferences for Professional Development

Workshops and conferences are invaluable for those seeking to transition into AI-resistant jobs. These professional events offer a unique blend of networking opportunities, hands-on learning experiences, and insights from industry leaders. The importance of such gatherings cannot be overstated, particularly in an ever-evolving job market.

Value of Attending Industry Events

Networking: One of the primary benefits of attending workshops and conferences is the opportunity to network. Engaging with peers, industry veterans, and potential employers can open doors to new career opportunities. Networking at these events enables professionals to:

- Build relationships with key industry players

- Exchange ideas and perspectives

- Discover job openings that may not be advertised publicly

Learning: Workshops and conferences often feature sessions led by experts who share cutting-edge knowledge and practices. This access to firsthand information helps attendees stay ahead in their fields. Key learning opportunities include:

- Exposure to the latest trends and technologies

- Practical demonstrations of new tools and methodologies

- Interactive sessions that encourage skill development

How to Choose Relevant Workshops

Choosing the right workshops can be daunting given the myriad options available. To make informed decisions, consider the following criteria:

Relevance: Ensure that the workshop aligns with your career goals and interests. For instance, if you aim to enhance your skills in data analysis, a workshop focusing on advanced Excel techniques or Python programming would be beneficial.

Speakers and Instructors: Research the credibility of the speakers or instructors. Renowned professionals bring a wealth of experience and can provide deep insights into their areas of expertise.

Format and Structure: Some people learn better through hands-on activities while others benefit more from lectures or panel discussions. Opt for a format that suits your learning style.

Cost vs. Benefit: Evaluate whether the cost of attending is justified by the potential benefits. Often, investing in high-quality workshops pays off through improved skills and better job prospects.

Real-Life Example: TechCrunch Disrupt Conference

TechCrunch Disrupt is a prime example of an event that offers immense value. Known for its focus on technology startups, this conference includes a variety of workshops led by influential figures in tech innovation.

> "Disrupt has been an eye-opener for me," says Jane Doe, a product manager at a leading tech firm. "The networking opportunities alone have helped me secure partnerships that were crucial for our company's growth."

Strategies for Maximizing Benefits

Attending workshops and conferences is only half the battle; maximizing their benefits requires proactive strategies:

- **Preparation:** Before attending, research topics covered and prepare questions.

- **Active Participation:** Engage actively during sessions—ask questions, participate in discussions.

- **Follow-Up:** Post-event follow-ups are crucial. Connect with speakers and fellow attendees via LinkedIn or email to solidify relationships.

Workshops and conferences serve as vital platforms for professional growth in AI-resistant roles. By carefully selecting relevant events and actively engaging in them, professionals can significantly enhance their skills, expand their networks, and stay updated with industry trends.

Real-world examples like TechCrunch Disrupt underscore how these events can catalyze career advancement by providing unparalleled learning experiences and networking opportunities.

Online Courses and E-Learning Platforms for Flexible Education

The digital age has changed how we learn, making online courses and e-learning platforms essential for developing skills. As we face the challenges of moving to jobs that can't be replaced by AI, these online tools offer unmatched flexibility and access.

Overview of Popular Online Learning Platforms

There are many e-learning platforms that cater to different learning needs, offering courses from basic skills to advanced technical knowledge. Here are some of the most popular platforms:

- **Coursera**: Partnering with top universities and organizations, Coursera offers courses in various fields, including technology, business, and humanities. Their specializations and professional certificates are highly regarded.

- **edX**: Founded by Harvard and MIT, edX provides high-quality courses from leading institutions worldwide. Their MicroMasters programs offer a pathway to advanced degrees.

- **Udacity**: Known for its "Nanodegree" programs, Udacity focuses on in-demand tech skills such as AI, data science, and programming. These courses are designed in collaboration with industry leaders like Google and IBM.

- **LinkedIn Learning**: Leveraging LinkedIn's professional network, this platform offers personalized course recommendations based on your career interests and goals.

- **Khan Academy**: While primarily aimed at K-12 education, Khan Academy also provides resources for higher education subjects and professional development.

Benefits of Online Courses for Skill Development

Engaging in online learning offers several advantages that are particularly relevant for those seeking to transition to AI-resistant roles:

1. **Flexibility**:

- *Self-paced Learning*: Online courses allow learners to progress at their own speed, accommodating different schedules and learning styles.

- *Anytime, Anywhere Access*: The ability to access course materials from any location at any time eliminates geographical barriers.

1. **Cost-effectiveness**:

- *Affordable Options*: Many e-learning platforms offer free or low-cost courses, making education more accessible without the burden of high tuition fees.

- *Financial Aid*: Platforms like Coursera and edX provide financial aid options for those who qualify, enhancing accessibility further.

1. **Wide Range of Courses**:

- *Diverse Subjects*: From coding bootcamps to leadership seminars, there's a course available for nearly every interest and career goal.

- *Updated Content*: Curricula are frequently updated to reflect the latest industry trends and technologies.

1. **Interactive Learning Experience**:

- *Multimedia Content*: Engaging videos, interactive quizzes, and hands-on projects enhance comprehension and retention.

- *Peer Collaboration*: Discussion forums and group projects facilitate networking with fellow learners globally.

1. **Credential Recognition**:

- *Certificates & Degrees*: Many platforms offer certificates upon course completion that can be added to resumes or LinkedIn profiles. Some even provide pathways to accredited degrees.

- *Employer Recognition*: Recognized certifications from reputable institutions can significantly boost employability.

Real-world Application

Consider Jane Doe, a mid-level marketing professional aiming to pivot into a data analytics role—a field less susceptible to automation due to its reliance on human interpretation. She enrolled in a series of Coursera courses on data science offered by Johns Hopkins University. Balancing her job with evening study sessions allowed her to gain expertise without disrupting her work life. Upon completion, she received a certification which played a pivotal role in securing her new position as a Data Analyst at a tech firm.

As Jane's story illustrates, online courses empower individuals by providing flexible educational opportunities tailored to evolving job market demands. The continuous evolution of these platforms ensures they remain relevant tools for lifelong learning.

By leveraging the vast array of resources available through e-learning platforms, professionals can equip themselves with the necessary skills to thrive in AI-resistant careers. This proactive approach not only enhances individual capabilities but also contributes significantly to organizational resilience in an era dominated by technological advancements.

Developing Leadership and Management Skills for Career Advancement in AI-Resistant Roles and Importance of Soft Skills Communication Skills in the Workplace

Importance of Leadership Capabilities in AI-Resistant Roles

Leadership skills are essential in navigating the complexities of AI-resistant jobs. As AI continues to automate routine tasks, the demand for exceptional leadership grows. Leaders are needed to inspire innovation, drive strategic initiatives, and manage multifaceted teams. The essence of leadership in this context is not just about overseeing tasks but about fostering a culture that thrives on human creativity and problem-solving.

Key Attributes of Effective Leaders:

- **Visionary Thinking:** Ability to foresee industry trends and adapt strategies accordingly.

- **Empathy:** Understanding team dynamics and individual motivations.

- **Decisiveness:** Making informed decisions swiftly in high-stakes situations.

Example: Satya Nadella, CEO of Microsoft, transformed the company by embracing a growth mindset, prioritizing empathy, and focusing on cloud computing—a decision that steered Microsoft toward unprecedented success.

Training Resources Available for Aspiring Leaders

To cultivate leadership skills, various resources can be utilized. These include online courses, mentorship programs, workshops, and literature on management theories. Investing time in these resources can significantly enhance one's ability to lead effectively.

Recommended Resources:

- **Online Courses:** *Coursera's "Inspirational Leadership"* by HEC Paris

- *edX's "Leadership Principles"* by Harvard Business School

- **Mentorship Programs:** *LinkedIn Career Advice*

- *MicroMentor*

- **Workshops:** *Dale Carnegie Training*

- *FranklinCovey Workshops*

Real-World Applications of Management Theories

Management theories offer a framework for understanding organizational behavior and implementing effective strategies. The application of these theories can be observed in various successful organizations.

Examples:

- **Theory X and Theory Y:** Google's approach aligns with Theory Y, which posits that employees are self-motivated and thrive under supportive management.

- **Maslow's Hierarchy of Needs:** Companies like Zappos prioritize employee well-being to ensure higher productivity and job satisfaction.

The Evolving Role of Soft Skills in the Workplace

Soft skills bridge the gap between technology and human interaction. In an era dominated by AI, these skills become even more crucial as they facilitate collaboration, conflict resolution, and emotional intelligence.

Essential Soft Skills:

- **Communication:** Clear articulation of ideas and active listening.

- **Teamwork:** Collaborative efforts towards common goals.

- **Adaptability:** Flexibility in adapting to new roles or challenges.

Quote: "Soft skills get little respect but will make or break your career." — Peggy Klaus

Strategies for Improving Communication Abilities

Effective communication is the cornerstone of professional success. Enhancing this skill requires practice and awareness of both verbal and non-verbal cues.

Techniques to Improve Communication:

1. **Active Listening:** Fully concentrating on what is being said rather than just passively hearing the message.

2. **Feedback Mechanisms:** Regularly seeking and providing constructive feedback.

3. **Public Speaking Courses:** Programs like Toastmasters can significantly improve public speaking abilities.

Example: Jeff Bezos emphasizes clear communication at Amazon by encouraging concise writing through structured documents instead of PowerPoint presentations during meetings.

Transitioning into AI-resistant roles necessitates a robust blend of leadership capabilities and soft skills. By investing in targeted training resources and continually honing communication abilities, professionals can navigate the evolving job landscape with confidence and resilience.